Susan Bivin Aller

Lerner Publications Company
Minneapolis

To the memory of my father,
born in Missouri on the banks of the Mississippi River
during Mark Twain's lifetime,
and to the promise of my grandson,
his namesake—David George Aller—
born nearly a century later in Paris
on the banks of another great river, the Seine—S.B.A.

A&E and **BIOGRAPHY** are trademarks of the A&E Television Networks, registered in the United States and other countries.

Some of the people profiled in this series have also been featured in A&E's acclaimed BIOGRAPHY series, which is available on videocassette from A&E Home Video. Call 1-800-423-1212 to order.

This book is available in two editions:
Library binding by Lerner Publications Company,
  a division of Lerner Publishing Group
Softcover by First Avenue Editions,
  an imprint of Lerner Publishing Group
241 First Avenue North
Minneapolis, MN 55401 U.S.A.

Website address: www.lernerbooks.com

Library of Congress Cataloging-in-Publication Data

Aller, Susan Bivin.
    Mark Twain / by Susan Bivin Aller.
      p.   c.m — (A&E biography)
    Includes bibliographical references and index.
    ISBN 0-8225-4994-8 (lib. bdg. : alk. paper)
    ISBN 0-8225-9696-2 (pbk. : alk. paper)
    1. Twain, Mark, 1835–1910—Juvenile literature. 2. Authors,
American—19th century—Biography—Juvenile literature. [1. Twain,
Mark, 1835–1910. 2. Authors, American.] I. Title. II. Series.
PS1331.A76   2001
818'.409—dc21   00-009561

Manufactured in the United States of America
1 2 3 4 5 6 – JR – 06 05 04 03 02 01

CONTENTS

This is the earliest known picture of Samuel Langhorne Clemens, who later became known to the world as Mark Twain. Here, the fifteen-year-old printer's apprentice proudly points to his name—SAM—on his belt buckle.

Chapter ONE

THE
APPRENTICE

THE RED-HAIRED BOY STOOD ON A WOODEN BOX TO reach the letters of metal type. He was small-boned, with delicate hands and feet, and his large, second-hand clothing covered him up like a circus tent. He chewed on a cigar and sang cheerfully as he worked.

This is how Mark Twain remembered himself as a twelve-year-old boy working as a printer's apprentice in Hannibal, Missouri.

He was not "Mark Twain" then. He was just plain Sam Clemens, "printer's devil" for the local newspaper, the *Missouri Courier,* and he cleaned up the office and delivered newspapers. He received no pay for his work, only the usual terms for a printer's apprentice in 1848: a place to sleep, board (food), and two suits of clothes. "More board than clothes," he remembered, "and not much of either."

Sam and the other apprentices slept on pallets on the office floor. When poor rations left them hungry, they would sneak down to the cellar for potatoes and onions, which they cooked on the office heating stove. Sam's clothes were the castoffs of his employer, Joseph Ament, who was twice the size of Sam.

Sam may have been small, but he had a large talent for getting into mischief. The window of the upstairs printing shop offered a fine view of the street. Once, Sam followed an irresistible urge to drop a watermelon shell on the head of his goody-goody brother Henry, who was passing by below. It was "a thing which I have been trying to regret for fifty-five years," he recorded in his autobiography.

Sam learned to be quick and accurate at picking out the letters from the type case and setting them into lines to make words and sentences. Before long, Mr. Ament gave him special typesetting jobs. Sam felt very important when he set type for the stories about the war in Mexico—fresh from the telegraph wire that had recently connected his small Missouri town to the outside world. Sometimes, when news was scarce, Sam made up some short items to fill the end of a column. These were his first attempts at fiction.

Sam liked his work. He decided that when he finished his apprenticeship and became a qualified printer, or journeyman, he would hire himself out to different papers and see the world by traveling from one job to another. Then the circus came to town, and he thought it might be more exciting to be a clown. Clowns traveled, too. Then the minstrel show and other performers arrived in Hannibal, and twelve-year-old Sam was stagestruck. He longed to be on stage with the actors. He got his chance when he volunteered to be hypnotized by a traveling mesmerizer. He pretended to be under the control of the hypnotist, and he ran from imaginary snakes, kissed imaginary girls, caught imaginary fish with an imaginary pole, and entertained with other antics. When the hypnotist stuck Sam with pins to prove that the boy was hypnotized, Sam had to pretend really hard and not show how much it hurt! Sam's performance made him famous that week. Maybe he would become an actor. "I was born excited," he wrote, remembering his many changes of career plans.

When he finished work at the newspaper office, Sam headed for the river to play or fish or swim with his friends. One day, he thought, he would head down that river on a steamboat to see the world and seek his fortune.

He did not know the river itself would be a source of that fortune. Printer, traveler, actor, clown—he would become all of them, and much, much more.

"I was postponed to Missouri," wrote Sam Clemens of his premature birth. Sam was born in this two-room house in Florida, Missouri, shortly after the family made the difficult move there from Tennessee in 1835.

Chapter TWO

AN AMERICAN BOYHOOD

IN THE SPRING OF **1835,** JOHN MARSHALL CLEMENS
and his wife, Jane Lampton Clemens, gathered their
four children, their slave girl, and their possessions
for a difficult journey. They were on their way
through Tennessee and Kentucky to the frontier state
of Missouri. Marshall Clemens was a tall, thin man in
his late thirties, stern and unsmiling, but respected for
his honesty and high principles.

In Tennessee, Marshall had practiced law for a while
and had run a general store. But he was unsuccessful
and lost most of his assets, including all but one of
the slaves he had inherited.

Then hope arrived—in the form of an invitation
from his brother-in-law John Quarles. More than a

year earlier, John and his wife, Patsy, who was Jane Clemens's favorite sister, had followed the tide of western migration. They wrote glowing letters from the new town of Florida, Missouri, on the Salt River. They urged Marshall and Jane to sell everything and join them in Missouri.

Marshall loaded his family and goods into an old carriage pulled by two horses. He and Jane rode in it with their three younger children: Pamela (pronounced *pam-EE-lah)* and Margaret, who were eight and five, and Benjamin, who was three. Ten-year-old Orion (pronounced *OH-ree-uhn)* and Jennie, their slave girl, rode on horseback. There had been another child, a baby boy born after Pamela, but he lay in a Tennessee grave.

Ahead lay hopes of success. John Quarles had offered Marshall a partnership in his general store at the main crossroads in the town of Florida. As the town's leading citizen, John was working to make the town grow by attracting steamboats and railroads and more settlers to it.

Marshall and Jane Clemens could hardly afford another child, but during the long westward move, Jane became pregnant again. Pretty red-haired Jane, with her high spirits and warm heart, was eager to help her husband make a fresh start. In her youth in Kentucky, she had been the most popular girl in town. She loved dancing and telling stories and going to parades and circuses. Maybe Marshall's luck would

A mural depicting the Clemens family arriving in Florida, Missouri, is displayed on the wall of the post office in the nearby town of Paris, Missouri.

change once they settled in Missouri, and Jane's stern, silent husband would become more sociable.

When they reached Florida, Missouri, in the summer of 1835, they found a frontier town of twenty log houses and about one hundred settlers. Marshall rented a simple two-room house. There, on November 30, the new baby arrived, two months prematurely. In the sky that night, Halley's Comet streaked toward the horizon. Jane, who believed in signs and superstitions, felt that the appearance of the comet was a good omen. The baby was tiny and feeble, but surely he would be special in some way—if he lived. So he was baptized with special names: Samuel for his Clemens grandfather, and Langhorne, to honor an old family friend. They called the baby Sammy or Little Sam.

Jane was determined Sammy would survive, and he did. But he was frail and sickly, so his mother dosed him with home remedies to cure the many illnesses he caught. The medicines tasted terrible, and when she wrapped him in wet sheets and laid socks full of hot ashes on him, Sammy felt as if he were being smothered. His mother called him "a sickly and precarious and tiresome and uncertain child."

Marshall Clemens spent what little money he had to buy land. There he planned to build a grand family house. He was elected a justice of the peace and after that was called "Judge" Clemens. Like John Quarles, Marshall became a leader in the tiny, optimistic town.

Jane and Marshall dreamed about becoming rich landowners, like their aristocratic Virginia and English ancestors had been. But Marshall Clemens was not a good businessman. His partnership with John Quarles fell apart, and his law practice didn't pay enough to support his family. Finally, all he could afford to build on the homestead were two single-room cabins joined together.

When Sam was two and a half, the Clemenses had another baby, whom they named Henry. A year later, in 1839, Sam's nine-year-old sister Margaret died of a sudden fever. By this time, neither the town of Florida nor Marshall Clemens was prospering. The family struggled with both poverty and grief.

Discouraged by his own failures, Marshall Clemens traded his property in Florida and much of his remaining cash for some land in the more promising town of Hannibal, Missouri. Then he moved his family thirty miles east to Hannibal, on the banks of the Mississippi River.

When Marshall and Jane Clemens arrived in Hannibal in 1839, they joined about sixty other families, most of whom were growing hogs, wheat, hemp, and tobacco. The town prospered. Barges and steamboats docked at Hannibal and carried goods to market all along "the great Mississippi, the majestic, the magnificent Mississippi, rolling its mile-wide tide along, shining in the sun."

Hannibal nestled in a curving riverbank. Points of land to the north and south framed a view of the water and the dense Illinois forest on the far side. Rutted, unpaved roads crossed the town and then climbed steeply away from the river into fields and wilderness.

Marshall's piece of land in the center of town contained a small hotel called the Virginia House and another building that was suitable for a store. He moved his family into the Virginia House. Then, using borrowed money, he stocked his store with merchandise.

In this engraving, Hannibal appears much as it did in Mark Twain's boyhood. Steamboats carry goods on the Mississippi River, and hills behind the town lead to the American wilderness.

He gave the job of clerk to his eldest son, Orion, almost fifteen, who was dreamy and bookish.

As for Little Sam, he continued to be the family's most troublesome child. He was very excitable and sometimes had convulsions. He walked in his sleep. Sometimes his family would find him in a dark corner, weeping with fear about his nightmares. And he continued to have periods of unexplained illness.

Sammy had an angelic appearance: tousled reddish hair, a sweet smile, and innocent gray-green eyes. He spoke in what his family called "Sammy's long talk," a slow, measured drawl he learned from his Kentucky-born mother. But his behavior was far from angelic.

Sammy started school when he was about five. He sometimes made trouble in class, but he became the school's champion speller. The only time he lost the medal for good spelling was when he misspelled "February" on purpose to let his best girlfriend, Laura Hawkins, win. Sammy was a favorite with the girls because he was sweet and gentle with them and made them laugh.

There was plenty for an imaginative boy like Sam to do with his young friends. They played endless games of Indians in the woods outside the town. They dug for pirate treasure. They waded and fished in the streams. They collected turtle eggs and other fascinating things. Once, when Sam's mother emptied his pockets, she found two fishhooks, a buckskin thong, marbles, a ball, a broken stick of chalk, and a wooden soldier with one leg.

Sam and his friends were fascinated by the river. From the time they were four or five years old, they had played at being steamboats—making clanging and hissing noises, marching forward and then back to imitate the great vessels that came in and out of Hannibal.

Most people in Hannibal took religion very seriously, including Sam's mother. Sam remembered his father going to church only once, but Jane insisted that her children regularly attend the Methodist Sunday school. Later, when she became a Presbyterian, they went to that church with her. The preachers frightened Sammy with their dramatic descriptions of what happened to people who were wicked. When a traveling evangelist preacher came through Hannibal and held large public revival meetings outdoors, Jane took the children to hear him. Little Sam was fascinated by the spectacle of crowds and loud singing and hand clapping. It scared him, too, and he watched in amazement as the preacher submerged sinners, who were seeking forgiveness, in the creek to baptize them.

Sammy believed he was wicked. He shivered in his bed during thunderstorms, repenting for all he was worth and expecting to be struck by lightning. "He didn't believe in Hell, but he was afraid of it."

By the time Sam was six, things were not going well with his family. Dreamy Orion was not especially skilled at managing the store, and the store failed. So Marshall sent his oldest son to work for a printer in St. Louis. Then Marshall began to practice law again.

In the spring of 1842, Sammy's brother Benjamin, who was nearly ten, died after a sudden illness. Six-year-old Sam looked on with shock as his mother knelt by the deathbed, moaning and weeping over the body of his brother.

Sam's mother desperately needed to get away from her gloomy husband and the near-poverty of life in Hannibal. The fortunes of her brother-in-law John Quarles had continued to rise, and he had moved his large family to a farm just outside the town of Florida. So that summer, Jane took Sammy, Pamela, and Henry to stay with Aunt Patsy and Uncle John on the Quarles farm.

It was the first of many idyllic summers in that "heavenly place for a boy."

A HEAVENLY PLACE FOR A BOY

Sammy found himself in the midst of a large and affectionate family—his aunt and uncle and eight cousins. Uncle John was a big, hearty man who joked with the children and told them stories. Aunt Patsy was a lively, sociable woman who gathered her large family on the great covered porch to eat the bountiful meals she and the slaves prepared. Sammy grew stronger and healthier as he feasted all summer on fried chicken, roast pig, turkey, rabbit, pheasant, biscuits, batter cakes, corn on the cob, buttermilk, dumplings, cobblers, and fresh fruits and vegetables from the fields and orchard.

He roamed barefoot with his cousins over the fascinating farm, exploring the smokehouse and stables and tobacco-curing house, learning how to ride a horse and how to pick the sweetest watermelon.

Sometimes Sammy was allowed to go 'possum and 'coon hunting with his cousins at night, led through the woods by the slaves carrying torches. When the dogs bayed, it signaled that the wild animal had run up a tree. Then everyone scrambled over roots and through briars to get to the spot, light a fire, and chop down the tree. "I remember it all well," he wrote, "and the delight every one got out of it, except the 'coon."

Behind the orchard, Uncle John's slave families lived in small log cabins. Through the trees, Sammy could see the lights of their fires and hear them singing. It was a magical world where Sammy felt safe and protected. He listened in wonder to the stories and music of the slaves. They came from many different homelands and spoke in a rich mix of West African, British, Caribbean, and American Southern dialects. He listened to and remembered their songs and their way of telling stories.

Sammy's special friend was gray-haired Uncle Dan'l, the head of one of the slave families. He was the warmhearted adviser and ally to all the children, but for Sammy in particular, he became a model for loyalty, generosity, and storytelling.

On "privileged nights," Uncle Dan'l let all the children—black and white together—sit around the hearth in his kitchen. He told them stories: magical, funny, scary folktales and legends. His voice rose and fell and enchanted them, with "the firelight playing on their faces and the shadows flickering upon the walls clear back toward the cavernous gloom of the rear." When the fire had nearly burned out, the children huddled close around Uncle Dan'l for the final story—the ghost story. "Once 'pon a time," it always began, and the old man would weave his hands through the shadows and wail and cry in the voice of the ghost. "Who-o-o got my golden arm?" The young audience shivered with delight, then nearly jumped out of their skins when he yelled out the last line. "YOU GOT IT!"

Then it was off to bed, and Sammy would climb to his room under the rafters, with echoes of "Who-o-o got my golden arm?" still in his ears.

As Sammy grew older and healthier, his capacity for mischief increased. He put garter snakes in Aunt Patsy's workbasket "for a surprise . . . and when they began to climb out of it, it disordered her mind."

To his mother, Sam would say, "there's something in my coat pocket for you." And when she put her hand in, she would pull it right out with a shiver. A bat! "It was remarkable, the way she couldn't learn to like private bats," Sam said.

Sam sensed that he was probably his mother's favorite child, even though he gave her a good deal of trouble. "I think she enjoyed it. She had no [trouble] at all with my brother Henry, who was two years younger than I, and I think that the unbroken monotony of his goodness and truthfulness and obedience

At the age of fifty-five, Sam's high-spirited, red-haired mother, Jane Lampton Clemens, was painted with a youthful band of flowers and ribbons in her hair.

would have been a burden to her but for the relief and variety which I furnished in the other direction."

LURED BY THE RIVER

At home in Hannibal, Sammy continued to annoy and frighten his mother. He played hooky from school, lied when he was caught, and tattled on Henry.

By the time he was nine or ten, he would climb out his bedroom window after dark when he heard a special catcall and slide down a shed roof. There he would meet his friends, including an older boy he much admired: Tom Blankenship, son of the town drunkard. Jane had forbidden Sam to play with Tom, but that just made the escape more exciting. Tom Blankenship never had to go to school or take a bath or do any of the other things Sam had to do. He knew all about hunting and trapping, how to ward off evil with spells and charms, and how to cure warts with dead cats.

A lot of the boys' nighttime adventures took place in the cemetery. Tom had dreams that told him where to find buried treasure. He made the younger boys dig for it while he leaned against a tree, smoking a corn-cob pipe and watching them.

Sam's closest friend, though, was Will Bowen. Together, the two played Robin Hood and pirates in caves and on Holliday's Hill above the river. "Now and then we had a hope that if we lived and were good, God would permit us to be pirates," Sam wrote.

Hannibal was a young, rough frontier town, and it was not uncommon for Sam to witness crimes and violent acts on the streets. One night after dark, he crept into his father's law office to avoid punishment for playing hooky from school. He lay down on a couch to sleep but was aware of something else in the room. As the night wore on, moonlight gradually revealed the body of a man who had been stabbed earlier in the day and carried to the law office to die. Wasting no time, Sam jumped out the window.

"I was not scared," Sam said, "but I was considerably agitated."

The slaves Sam knew on Uncle John Quarles's farm

were treated well, but on the streets of Hannibal, Sam often saw the cruel, dark side of slavery. Once, he saw a slave die in agony after his master struck him with a rock.

Sam was sickened when he saw a group of black men and women chained together and lying on the pavement, waiting to be shipped down the river and sold on the slave market. "Those were the saddest faces I have ever seen," he wrote.

The mighty river that flowed past Hannibal attracted Sam more and more, but like the town, the river held both pleasure and terror for the boy. He knew that people could drown in the dangerous currents and drop-offs. Even though all the boys could swim, two of Sam's young friends lost their lives while swimming in the river.

Sam himself was rescued from drowning twice, once by a man and once by a girl, both slaves. His frightened mother comforted herself by remarking there wasn't much danger. "People who are born to be hanged are safe in the water," she joked.

He and his friends often swam out into the river to hitch a ride on a great barge or keelboat loaded with cargo that was being floated downstream to New Orleans. Sam was fascinated by the rude manners and colorful language of the crews. He watched the boasting, brawling, drunken raftsmen and listened to their loud yells. One of them "jumped up in the air and cracked his heels together again and shouted out:

Steamboats brought excitement, traveling entertainment, and commerce to towns along the Mississippi River. Sam and his friends dreamed of becoming steamboat pilots.

'Whoo-oop! I'm the old original iron-jawed, brass-mounted, copper-bellied corpse-maker from the wilds of Arkansaw!' "

Steamboats were even more exciting to watch. Most carried goods and passengers, but others were dressed up as showboats. These floating gilded palaces, loud with the music of calliopes and bands, brought singers, dancers, minstrels—and the seamier world of gamblers, prostitutes, and charlatans—to towns along the river. A gaudy procession of circuses, theater troupes, magicians, mind readers, con artists, and frauds also arrived in the river towns. Sam Clemens saw it all.

When Sam was nine years old, he hid himself under a boat on the top deck of a steamboat and sailed downriver on it. He was soon discovered, however, and put off at the next stop, where relatives took him back to his family and—no doubt—to swift punishment. It didn't cure Sam of his firm decision, shared by most of his friends, to become a steamboat man when he grew up.

The wharf at Hannibal was generally quiet and deserted. But when the cry "steamboat-a-comin!" rang out, the town burst alive with sound and action.

"Drays, carts, men, boys, all go hurrying from many quarters to a common center, the wharf. . . . People fasten their eyes upon the coming boat as upon a wonder they are seeing for the first time. . . . The furnace doors are open and the fires glaring bravely; the upper decks are black with passengers; the captain stands by the big bell, calm, imposing, the envy of all."

After a few minutes of extreme noise and activity,

passengers and freight unloaded and loaded, "the steamer is under way again. . . . After ten more minutes the town is dead again, and the town drunkard asleep by the skids once more."

When Sam was eleven, his father caught pneumonia after a long horseback ride through a March sleet storm. Jane called Orion back from his printer's job in St. Louis to help out. Two weeks later, with his family at his bedside, Marshall Clemens died at the age of forty-eight.

"He put his arm around my sister's neck," Sam remembered, "and kissed her, saying, 'Let me die.' . . . In all my life, up to that time, I had never seen one member of the Clemens family kiss another one."

Sam spent the next several years getting an education in the "poor boys' college" of working as a printer and traveling around the country. Here he is at age eighteen.

Chapter **THREE**

TOOLS OF THE TRADE

AT HIS FATHER'S DEATHBED, SAMMY STOOD AND wept as his mother asked him to make a promise.

"I will promise anything, if you won't make me go to school! Anything!"

"Only promise me to be a better boy," she said simply. "Promise not to break my heart!"

Jane and Sammy both knew the odds were against his keeping that promise for long. He wanted to be serious and industrious, but he had in him a good deal of his mother's merry, mischievous nature.

Marshall Clemens had died with few assets, and it quickly became clear to Jane and Orion that the family needed money urgently. Orion returned to his job in St. Louis, where he earned enough to send home three dollars a week. Pamela helped by giving guitar and piano lessons, and Jane took in boarders.

Sam and Henry continued to go to school, while their mother struggled in near-poverty to feed and clothe the family. When Sam was twelve, the age at which most boys were sent out to learn a trade, he was sent to be a live-in apprentice with Joseph Ament. Ament was the printer and owner of Hanni-

In a print shop much like this, Sam Clemens lived and worked as an apprentice for two years.

bal's newspaper, the *Missouri Courier*. Sam's carefree childhood had come to an abrupt end.

At Ament's shop, Sam learned how to hand-set words—lining up individual letters of metal type. His good spelling helped him to work accurately. He felt how much words weighed in his hands and saw how they fit together in a form to become printed pages. He also learned that the quicker a printer turned out pages of type, the more money he earned.

Toward the end of Sam's apprenticeship, Orion moved back to Hannibal, borrowed money, and bought his own newspaper. When his apprenticeship ended, Sam went to work for his brother.

As Sam walked along the street one day, he reached down to pick up a piece of paper that fluttered down in front of him. It was the page of a book about Joan of Arc. Sam knew almost nothing about history and had never heard of the French peasant girl who led an army to victory. But the story of her heroism moved him so much that he decided to read more about Joan of Arc. From that, he continued a hungry study of history.

The more Sam read, the more he wanted to read. He began to study German with the local shoemaker. Then his reading gave him ideas for articles and stories, and he asked Orion if he could write some for the paper. But the Hannibal paper had only a small, local audience, and Sam wanted greater things. So he wrote some articles about Hannibal for newspapers in

Boston and Philadelphia. He was thrilled when they were printed over his initials "S.L.C." He was sixteen years old, and two East Coast newspapers had paid him for his writing!

Every time Orion went out of town on short business trips, he left Sam in charge. This gave Sam the chance to use his well-developed talent for story-telling, comedy, and satire to liven up the paper.

"Terrible Accident! 500 men killed and missing!!!" shouted a headline Sam wrote once when Orion was away. Underneath, he printed in smaller type: "We had set the above head up, expecting (of course) to use it, but as the accident hasn't happened, yet, we'll say (To be Continued)."

Apparently subscribers appreciated the change, because circulation increased during Orion's absences. This must have been gratifying, although new subscriptions weren't often paid in hard cash but in turnips and firewood.

By the spring of 1853, seventeen-year-old Sam had grown weary of such work. Orion couldn't afford to pay Sam any salary, so although he was now a qualified printer, Sam was still working like an unpaid apprentice. He wanted to get away.

He told his mother he was going to St. Louis to work as a journeyman printer for a few months. He would stay with his sister Pamela, who had recently married a prosperous St. Louis merchant named Will Moffett. Sam's real goal was to go to New York City and see the Crystal Palace at the first World's Fair. After two months in St. Louis, he headed for New York.

JOURNEYMAN PRINTER

While he was in New York, Sam worked in a printing office and kept on reading, going to a printers' library in the evenings. By the first of October, Sam was ready to move on. He worked night shifts in Philadelphia for a while. Then he headed to Washington, D. C. After a year away from his family, Sam returned for a visit. While he was away, Orion had sold out in Hannibal and moved to Muscatine, Iowa, where he ran another newspaper. He had taken his mother, Jane, and his younger brother, Henry, to live with him.

Soon afterward, Orion married and, at his bride Mollie's insistence, moved to her hometown of Keokuk, Iowa, where he bought another newspaper. Jane decided to leave the newlyweds alone and went to St. Louis to live with Pamela. Orion, needing

Orion Clemens, ten years older than his brother Sam, bought small newspapers and hired Sam to work for him—but never paid him.

cheap, reliable labor, urged Sam and Henry to come work for him in Keokuk. They did, and Sam entertained himself there by taking dancing lessons and leading an active social life. He had a good singing voice, and he could play the piano and guitar fairly well. The young ladies were attracted to his good looks and happy nature.

At a printers' banquet in Keokuk, Sam gave his first humorous after-dinner speech. When he stood up and began to string together rough jokes in his drawling "long talk," his fellow printers roared with laughter. For Sam, this was more fun than his performance with the hypnotist back in Hannibal.

In all, Sam spent about ten years as a printer. These traveling years working in printing shops and newspapers became for him, as they did for Benjamin Franklin, Abraham Lincoln, Walt Whitman, and many others, "the poor boys' college."

Sam saw different parts of the country, and he met many kinds of people. He lived in boardinghouses and hotels. He sometimes went hungry and sometimes had enough to spend on luxuries or entertainment. But most of all, Sam read and read and read: classics, poetry, history, astronomy, and geography. He read stories written for the newspapers he worked on, he edited them for publication, and he wrote page after page to fill out the newspaper columns.

"One isn't a printer ten years," Sam later observed, "without setting up acres of good and bad literature, and learning . . . to discriminate between the two . . . and meanwhile . . . consciously acquiring what is called a 'style.'"

Restless once more, Sam decided he would go to Brazil, where, he had heard, it was easy to make a fortune. In Cincinnati, Ohio, he boarded a steamship heading south.

PILOT ON THE PROUD MISSISSIPPI

On the way downriver, Sam remembered his boyhood dream of becoming a Mississippi steamboat pilot. At the wheel of the steamship *Paul Jones* stood one of the great pilots of the river, Horace Bixby. Only nine years older than Sam, Bixby, at thirty-one, had a dozen years of experience behind him and was fully licensed on the Ohio and Mississippi Rivers. He had an explosive temper and expected perfection from any cub pilots learning from him.

As luck would have it, Horace Bixby was nursing a sore foot when Sam embarked that winter day. Before long, Sam talked his way into the pilot's house and helped steer while Bixby rested his foot. Bixby, it turned out, knew Will Bowen, Sam's boyhood friend from Hannibal, who was piloting another steamboat on the river. It was a good reference.

"I planned a siege against my pilot," Sam said, "and at the end of three hard days he surrendered. He agreed to teach me the Mississippi River from New Orleans to St. Louis for five hundred dollars, payable out of the first wages I should receive after graduating. I entered upon the small enterprise of 'learning' twelve or thirteen hundred miles of the great Mississippi River with the easy confidence of my time of life. If I had really known what I was about to require of my faculties, I should not have had the courage to begin."

So instead of continuing on to Brazil, Sam went back upriver. On the return trip from New Orleans to St. Louis, Sam worked as the new cub. He recorded in his memory—and in his small notebook—thousands of details he would need to know in order to earn his coveted pilot's license and navigate the great Mississippi. He memorized the names of islands, towns, bends, and sandbars.

He was feeling quite cocky about how much he knew when Bixby asked him the shape of a certain bend in the river. Sam said he didn't know it had any particular shape.

Bixby exploded. Everything on the riverbanks had a shape, Bixby said. The only way a pilot could tell where he was or how to steer clear was to learn the shape by heart. Daylight was one thing, but at night— whether in full moonlight or in mist or rain—the shape looked entirely different, so only his memory of it would get him by safely.

Sam said he figured he had to try to load all that information into his head, even though the heavy cargo was sure to make him stoop-shouldered.

Just then, another pilot called to Bixby to tell him to watch out. The banks of an island upstream were caving in and the shoreline didn't look at all as it did before. Sam's spirits were down in the mud again. Even when he learned the shapes, they would change without warning!

Steamboats also needed to keep clear of the shallow parts of the river—less than nine or ten feet of water and they would hit bottom. Before electronic instruments, the depth of the river ahead of the boat was measured by men who dropped weighted lines into the water. The men boomed out the numbers: Deep four! Mark three! Quarter less three! Half twain! MARK TWAIN! Mark twain—meaning two fathoms (twelve feet of water)—was the boundary between water deep enough and water too shallow for a steamboat. If the numbers called out by the leadsmen were increasing, all was clear sailing. But if the numbers were going down, mark twain was an ominous warning to head for deeper, safer water.

Becoming a pilot took all the discipline Sam could muster. Horace Bixby was a hard taskmaster, furious when his cub made mistakes. He roared at Sam, "When I say I'll learn a man the river, I mean it. And you can depend on it, I'll learn him or kill him." Sam nearly quit several times.

Though grand and beautiful, steamboats held within their boilers the frightening possibility of catastrophe. No one could predict when a steamboat boiler might

explode. The riverbed was littered with steamboat car-
casses. Cheaply constructed and often overfired to
race against each other in reckless contests, steamboats survived only four or five years—if their boilers
didn't blow up first. Others ran aground in the dan-
gerously shifting river channels.

Sam was finishing his first year of training when
Bixby temporarily assigned him to work with the pilot
of the *Pennsylvania*. The pilot was a tyrannical and
malicious man named Brown. Sam had arranged for
his nineteen-year-old brother Henry to work as a clerk
on the same boat and was pleased to see his brother
starting on a promising career. Brown couldn't stand
Sam, and he eventually took out his anger on young
Henry by aiming for his head with a large lump of
coal. Sam ran between them with a heavy stool
and knocked Brown to the floor, then jumped on him
and beat him. As a result of the fight, Sam was transferred to another boat, but Henry remained with the
Pennsylvania.

Shortly afterward, the *Pennsylvania*'s boilers exploded, and Henry was fatally burned. Sam never for-
gave himself—he always felt partly responsible for
Henry's death.

But Sam continued his training. "The face of the
water, in time, became a wonderful book," he said, "a
book that was a dead language to the uneducated
passenger, but which told its mind to me without
reserve. . . . There was never a page that was void of

Henry Clemens, two years younger than his brother Sam, joined his brother at work on the steamboats.

interest." In 1859, two years after he began training, Sam earned his pilot's license. He had, indeed, learned the river.

Life as a pilot suited Sam perfectly. It was not dirty or physically taxing. He began to wear spotless white trousers, a long blue jacket, a fancy striped shirt, and patent-leather shoes. He grew side-whiskers to look more mature than his twenty-three years. And he brushed his unruly reddish hair high on top so he would appear taller. As pilot, he was absolute ruler of the boat once it was under way. Even the captain couldn't contradict him then.

A pilot earned $250 a month at a time when a preacher might work six months for the same amount. Sam felt it was a princely salary. Since he didn't have to pay rent or buy food on a steamboat,

In 1859, Samuel Clemens earned his license to be a steamboat pilot "on the Mississippi River to and from St. Louis and New Orleans."

Sam could send money home to his mother as well as indulge in pleasures for himself.

Eager groups gathered in the pilot-association rooms to hear Sam tell his humorous yarns. He continued to experiment with a drawling, sober-faced delivery, as he had with his printer friends, and he became a favorite along the river.

Sam had become an avid reader. He spent hours learning French and reading history, travel, and science books. He read Shakespeare and Byron, Sir Walter

Scott and John Bunyan. He studied astronomy, inspired by nights in the pilot's house watching the stars move in the sky.

Then suddenly this idyllic life came to an end. In April 1861, Confederate (Southern) troops fired on Fort Sumter in the harbor at Charleston, South Carolina. Southern slaveholding states seceded from the United States. President Abraham Lincoln called for troops to preserve the Union, and the Civil War began in earnest. The Mississippi River, a lifeline for troops and supplies, was abruptly closed to nonmilitary traffic.

Growing up in Missouri, bordered by both the North and the South, and traveling as he did in both the North and the South along the river, Sam couldn't decide which side to support. But he couldn't remain on the river. Sam's career as a pilot was over.

After visiting his mother and sister in St. Louis, Sam went to see old school friends in Hannibal. They talked him into joining the Confederate cause.

Politics in Missouri were confusing. Even though it was a slaveholding state, it remained part of the Union. Yet there was threat of invasion by Union troops. Sam was not particularly convinced that either side was right. But he was glad for the chance to have a good time with his boyhood friends. Everyone thought the war would be over in a few months at most.

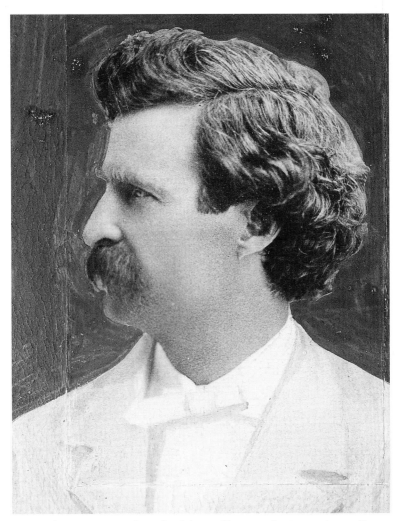

Sam Clemens once described himself as "5 ft. 8½ inches tall; weight about 145 pounds . . . dark brown hair and red moustache, full face with very high ears and light gray beautiful beaming eyes and a damned good moral character."

Chapter **FOUR**

LIGHTING OUT FOR THE TERRITORY

LIEUTENANT **SAMUEL** **CLEMENS,** **RIDING** **A** **STUBBORN** mule called Paint Brush, headed out with a dozen other members of the Marion Rangers to find the regular Confederate army. Local farmers had outfitted Sam and his friends—mostly Hannibal schoolmates from Marion County—for war. Sam's military equipment consisted of the mule, a pair of blankets, a homemade quilt, a frying pan, a small suitcase, an overcoat, an old rifle, twenty yards of rope, and an umbrella.

Only a month earlier, Sam had been the elegantly attired master of his universe, piloting a Mississippi steamboat.

Starting from Hannibal, the Rangers moved forward

only at night, to avoid Union patrols. They headed for the Salt River near the town of Florida, where they hoped to join the regular Confederate troops. But Northern sympathizers chased them away and set dogs on them. When drenching rains came, nobody would obey orders to stand guard in the rain. Finally, Sam had to walk because he developed a saddle boil and couldn't even ride his detested mule.

Rumors that Union troops were heading toward them put the Rangers into full retreat. Sam wrote that he knew more about retreating than the man who invented retreating.

They bedded down in a hayloft to sleep one night, and a comrade accidentally set fire to the hay with his pipe. Sam quickly rolled away from the fire and fell out the window onto the ground, nearly breaking his ankle. As a final insult, the others forked the burning hay out the window, and it landed right on him!

By this time, the Marion Rangers had lost their taste for army life, and they disbanded. They had been soldiers for all of two weeks. Sam stayed at a farmhouse until his saddle sores and sprained ankle healed. Then, afraid he would be shot as a deserter, he hid out with Orion and Mollie in Iowa.

In July 1861, Sam and Orion boarded a stagecoach bound for Nevada. There, Orion had a new job as territorial secretary, the assistant to the territorial governor. Sam was to be Orion's private secretary. The tired horses were exchanged for fresh ones every ten miles or so, but the passengers were not given time to change, shave, or bathe. More than once, a Pony Express rider passed them, galloping by with his precious packet of mail. Twenty days later, the stagecoach arrived in Carson City, Nevada Territory. Sam and Orion had traveled almost nonstop.

THE PONY EXPRESS

HERE HE COMES!"

Every neck is stretched further, and every eye strained wider. Away across the endless dead level of the prairie a black speck appears against the sky, and it is plain that it moves. Well, I should think so! In a second or two it becomes a horse and rider, rising and falling, rising and falling—sweeping toward us nearer and nearer—growing more and more distinct, more and more sharply defined—nearer and still nearer, and the flutter of the hoofs comes faintly to the ear—another instant a whoop and a hurrah from our upper deck [of the stagecoach], a wave of the rider's hand, but no reply, and man and horse burst past our excited faces, and go winging away like a belated fragment of a storm!

So sudden is it all, and so like a flash of unreal fancy, that but for the flake of white foam left quivering and perishing on a mail-sack after the vision had flashed by and disappeared, we might have doubted whether we had seen any actual horse and man at all, maybe.

from *Roughing It*

Sam didn't have much work to do for Orion, so he looked for some excitement. He spent several months prospecting for silver, panning for gold, and buying shares in claims that other miners swore were sure things. Sam went broke trying to strike it rich.

At night on the slopes of the Sierra Nevada, in the flimsy cabin he shared with several fellow miners, Sam began to write articles about his experiences. He sent them to the newspaper *Territorial Enterprise* in Virginia City and to other papers in Nevada and California. He signed these articles "Josh." But they didn't bring much money, and Sam was desperately looking for a way to support himself.

Finally, the editor of the *Territorial Enterprise,* Joseph Goodman, offered Sam twenty-five dollars a week to join his staff. Twenty-five dollars wasn't exactly a steamboat pilot's pay, but Sam was practically penniless. He didn't even have enough money to hire a horse, so he shouldered a heavy blanket roll filled with his possessions and started walking the 130 miles from his mining camp at Aurora to Virginia City. On a hot day in September, Sam limped into the newspaper's office and dropped into a chair.

"My starboard leg seems to be unshipped," he announced. "I think I'm falling to pieces."

He wore a faded flannel shirt with trousers tucked into his boots. A dirty slouch hat covered reddish hair that fell to his shoulders, and his long beard was stained with dust. He asked to see the editor.

Who was this? the startled subeditor wanted to know.

"My name is Clemens, and I've come to write for the paper."

On February 3, 1863, six months after starting work on the *Enterprise*, Sam signed a humorous travel article with the name Mark Twain. It stuck. People began calling him Mark Twain.

On February 3, 1863, in the composing room of the Territorial Enterprise, *Sam Clemens first signed the name Mark Twain to one of his articles.*

Sam Clemens had certainly heard mark twain called out many times on the Mississippi River. His choice of it as his pen name may have been simply that he liked the sound of it. Maybe it reminded him of the best job he had ever had. Also, the uncertain boundary between safety and danger fascinated him.

Twain means two or twin, and many of his stories and novels deal with look-alikes or actual twins. Some people think that Sam got the idea for his pen name when he frequented saloons in Nevada, where mark twain meant two drinks on credit. He certainly heard it often there, too.

Mark Twain loved wearing fancy clothes and being recognized on the streets of Virginia City. He had grown to be a young man of medium height and spare build, with narrow, sloping shoulders and delicate hands. One of those hands usually held a cigar. His intense gray-green eyes attracted people's attention and so did the thick eyebrows and unruly reddish hair above them. He moved in a circle of rowdy, drinking, gambling writers, entertainers, and traveling actors.

Eventually, Twain grew restless in the small town of Virginia City. He loved to visit San Francisco, California—attracted by its restaurants, hotels, theaters, and crowds—and he finally moved there. He got a job at the newspaper the *Morning Call*.

It wasn't long, however, before he and his friend at the *Call*, Steve Gillis, found themselves in trouble for

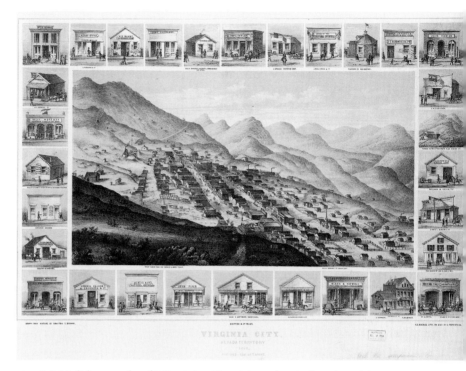

An 1861 lithograph of Virginia City, Nevada, is bordered by images of buildings in the town. Mark Twain worked in the Territorial Enterprise *office,* top row, fourth from the right.

various disturbances they caused. They left town and went to look for gold in the Sierra foothills near Jackass Hill, where Steve's two brothers had a cabin.

In good weather, the men took pans and shovels to the hills, hoping to wash a few nuggets free. When the weather was bad, they sat around the fire and told stories or read books.

Twain later spent four cold, wet weeks at a larger settlement called Angel's Camp, in Calaveras County, where he still had no luck finding gold. But the stories and characters he discovered at Jackass Hill and at Angel's Camp turned into a rich lode.

Chief among these nuggets was a funny little tale he heard at a tavern in Angel's Camp. It was about a fellow named Jim Smiley, who boasted that his frog could out-jump any frog in the county.

HIGH SEAS

Sam returned to San Francisco to work on the newspaper. But the excitement had gone out of it, and he felt hopelessly trapped. In October he wrote to Orion that he was utterly miserable. He concluded that if the Almighty had given him only one talent, for literature "of a low order—i.e. humorous," then he should already have begun "seriously scribbling to excite the laughter of God's creatures."

When a local editor published a bitter personal attack against him, Sam fell into deep depression. Not a moment too soon, the *Sacramento Union* asked Mark Twain to be a foreign correspondent in Hawaii. The Hawaiian Islands, not yet part of the United States, were called the Sandwich Islands. In March 1866, supplied with cigars, brandy, and introductions from friends, Twain embarked on the steamship *Ajax*.

The eleven-day journey from San Francisco to the Sandwich Islands furnished enough material for the first articles Twain wrote for the *Union*. He intended to stay only a month, but he found the islands and their people so captivating that he stretched his visit to four months.

His travel articles, twenty-five in all, entertained a wide audience. For the first time, many readers learned about the natural beauty, history, and economic opportunities of the Sandwich Islands.

He made a night visit to the live volcano of Kilauea and concluded his dramatic description with the kind of punch line his readers loved: The crater floor "was as black as ink . . . but over a mile square of it was ringed and streaked and striped with a thousand branching streams of liquid and gorgeously brilliant fire! . . . The smell of sulphur is strong, but not unpleasant to a sinner."

During Twain's months in the Sandwich Islands, Anson Burlingame, the U.S. minister to China, stopped by on his way to his post. The two men liked each other at once, and the diplomat gave the young journalist some fatherly advice: "I believe you have genius. What you need now is the refinement of association. Seek companionship among men of superior intellect and character. Refine yourself and your work. Never affiliate with inferiors; always climb."

The next day, word came that a lifeboat carrying fifteen starving men had landed on the island of Hawaii after forty-three days at sea. They were survivors of an American ship that had burned at sea.

Burlingame arranged for Twain to interview the survivors in the hospital. Twain hastily wrote a story, and a messenger tossed it onto the deck of a ship bound for the United States just as it sailed the next morning. Since ships were the only communications link between the Sandwich Islands and the mainland, Twain's story scooped other newspapers by being the first report of the disaster.

By the time Twain returned to San Francisco in August 1866, he found that his letters to the *Sacramento Union* had been printed in other newspapers. People across the country were beginning to recognize the name Mark Twain. Except for his friends in the West, no one knew that Mark Twain was the pseudonym of Sam Clemens.

Sam decided to give a lecture about his Hawaiian journey. There was quick money in platform lectures. So he rented a hall and printed a bill advertising the event. The ad also trumpeted the news that a splendid orchestra, a den of ferocious wild beasts, magnificent fireworks, and a grand torchlight procession—would NOT be appearing, for a variety of reasons. It concluded with the line "Doors open at 7 o'clock. The Trouble to begin at 8 o'clock."

As he walked on stage, Twain was gripped by an attack of stage fright so intense that he thought he saw the face of death. Somehow, he managed to shuffle to the platform and begin to read his lecture. He began to speak in his sober-faced, deadpan "long talk."

Minutes later, the audience was in the palm of his hand. He told them all about the wonders of the Sandwich Islands. He regaled them with hilarious descriptions of people and events. At the end, his laughing, gasping audience rewarded Mark Twain with an explosion of applause.

Here was a sure career! Elated by his success and the money he was raking in, Twain repeated his lecture more than a dozen times in the West. He moved on to the Midwest and finally made a triumphant debut in the Great Hall of Cooper Union in New York City. The reviews established Mark Twain as one of the new stars of the traveling lecture circuit. People filled halls to hear traveling lecturers, and Twain was one of the best. His unique style of delivery moved audiences to helpless laughter, awe, and tears.

In May 1867, Mark Twain's first book was published, the story of the frog he had heard in the West. The originality of Twain's humor propelled his name to national fame. *The Celebrated Jumping Frog of Calaveras County and Other Sketches* had a frog embossed in gold on the cover. The proud author felt that the golden frog alone was worth the price of the book.

A few months later, the San Francisco paper *Alta California* hired Mark Twain to be a traveling correspondent to Europe and the Holy Land. The excursion he joined was being organized by members of Plymouth Church in Brooklyn, New York, and would have a religious theme.

THE CELEBRATED JUMPING FROG

Simon Wheeler backed me into a corner and block-aded me there with his chair, and then sat me down and reeled off the monotonous narrative which follows this paragraph. He never smiled, he never frowned, he never changed his voice from the gentle-flowing key to which he tuned the initial sentence, he never betrayed the slightest suspicion of enthusiasm. . . .

"There was a feller here once by the name of Jim Smiley. . . he was the curiousest man about always betting on any thing that turned up you ever see, if he could get any body to bet on the other side; and if he couldn't he'd change sides. Any way that suited the other man would suit him—any way just so's he got a bet, he was satisfied.

"Well, thish-yer Smiley had rat-tarriers, and chicken cocks, and tom-cats, and all them kind of things, till you couldn't rest, and you couldn't fetch nothing for him to bet on but he'd match you. He ketched a frog one day, and took him home, and said he cal'klated to edercate him; and so he never done nothing for three months but set in his back yard and learn that frog to jump. And you bet you he did learn him, too. He'd give him a little punch behind, and the next minute you'd see that frog whirling in the air like a doughnut—see him turn one summer-set, or may be a couple, if he got a good start, and come down flat-footed and all right, like a cat. . . .

"Why, I've seen him set Dan'l Webster down here on this floor—Dan'l Webster was the name of the frog—and sing out, 'Flies, Dan'l, flies!' and quicker'n you could wink, he'd spring straight up, and snake a fly off'n the counter there, and flop down on the floor again as solid as a gob of mud, and fall to scratching the side of his head as indifferent as if he han't no idea he's been doin' any more'n any frog might do. You never see a frog so modest and straightfor'ard as he was, for all he was so gifted. . . . "

from *The Celebrated Jumping Frog of Calaveras County*

THE INNOCENTS ABROAD

Twain sailed from New York on the steamship *Quaker City*. He discovered, to his dismay, who his traveling companions were to be for the next five months: well-to-do, nondrinking, mostly middle-aged church members on a religious pilgrimage. Into this dignified group came Mark Twain, with his rough frontier humor, two cases of champagne, and a large supply of cheap cigars. On the first night of the cruise, Twain reported, the passengers' idea of pleasure was to hold a prayer meeting. Any other pleasure cruise would have had cards and dancing.

Before the Civil War, relatively few Americans had traveled abroad for pleasure. So when Twain wrote about the sights of Europe and the Holy Land with humor and satire, he gave his readers a fresh American look at the Old World. He wrote: "I used to worship the mighty genius of Michael Angelo . . . . But I do not want Michael Angelo for breakfast—for luncheon—for dinner—for tea—for supper. . . . In Genoa, he designed every thing. . . . In Florence, he painted every thing. . . . In Pisa he designed every thing but the old shot-tower, and they would have attributed that to him if it had not been so awfully out of the perpendicular. . . . I never felt . . . so filled with a blessed peace, as I did yesterday when I learned that Michael Angelo was dead."

In spite of the teasing, Twain took serious note of everything he experienced on the trip. He also listened with delight to the many new languages he heard. With what might be called a "phonographic memory," he remembered the sounds and rhythms of each, as he had with the dialects of the American South and West. "I listened as one who receives a revelation," he wrote.

Sam thought about Anson Burlingame's advice to refine his style. He decided this five-month voyage with upper-middle-class Easterners was a good place to start climbing the social ladder.

While on board, he found at least two fellow passengers with whom to develop friendships. One of these was Mary Fairbanks, wife of the owner of the *Cleveland Herald,* who took Sam into her circle. He saw in Mrs. Fairbanks a mother figure who would willingly help him learn social graces and manners. He began to call her "Mother," and she called him her "cub." She was also a journalist—on assignment from her husband's paper—and gave Sam advice on refining his writing, as well as his manners.

Mrs. Fairbanks knew the family of another passenger on board, seventeen-year-old Charley Langdon from Elmira, New York. She drew him into her circle along with Sam. Charley's parents were sending him on the trip to broaden his education before he took over the family's prosperous coal business. Some time during the trip, Charley showed Sam a small portrait painted on ivory. It was of Charley's older sister Olivia, and Sam fell in love with her at first sight. He saw in

This miniature painting of Olivia Langdon captured Sam's heart from the moment he saw it.

the portrait not only a pretty and rich young woman, but also an intelligent and educated one who might measure up to his ideal of a companion and wife. Sam Clemens had lived a vagabond life ever since leaving Hannibal at the age of seventeen. At the age of thirty-one, it was time to think about settling down.

Three great American humorists—Josh Billings, Mark Twain, and Petroleum V. Nasby—met in 1869 while all were on tour lecturing. Traveling lectures provided popular entertainment to audiences across the United States in the years following the Civil War.

Chapter FIVE

A GILDED LIFE

A FEW *QUAKER CITY* PASSENGERS MET FOR A NEW Year's reunion in New York City, and Charley Langdon brought along his sister Olivia and his father, Jervis Langdon. One night, Sam Clemens ate dinner with the Langdons, and afterward they went to Steinway Hall to hear a reading by the famous English author Charles Dickens. By the time the evening was over, Sam's fate was sealed. He had truly fallen in love with Olivia. Forty years later he said, "From that day to this she has never been out of my mind."

Mark Twain's letters from the *Quaker City* cruise were printed in the *Alta California* and in two New York papers. Elisha Bliss, owner of the American Publishing Company in Hartford, Connecticut, read them.

Bliss wrote Twain to ask if he would consider printing a collection of these letters in book form. Bliss's firm sold books by subscription, using an army of aggressive door-to-door salesmen to sell advance subscriptions to books that had not yet been written. The advance sales determined how many copies would be printed. Authors received their payments based on the price of the book: the larger the book, the higher the price and the greater the amount paid to the author. Twain liked the idea very much.

Twain went to Hartford to make arrangements with Bliss. While he was there, he also met the handsome, athletic, Yale-educated Joseph Twichell. Twichell was minister of the new Asylum Hill Congregational Church, which Twain nicknamed "The Church of the Holy Speculators" because of its wealthy congregation. Twain had long ago stopped going to church and generally disliked preachers. But Joseph Twichell was different. Unlike the Hannibal preachers of Twain's youth, Twichell didn't try to scare or convert people. Twichell accepted people as they were, including Twain with his bawdy sense of humor and rough manners. From their first meeting, Twichell's friendship grew to serve as both a rock and a well of inspiration for Twain. Twain began to think that Hartford would be an ideal place to live.

In August, Sam visited Olivia Langdon in Elmira, New York. Afterward he launched a letter-writing campaign to win her. In succeeding months, he arranged several more visits to see her. But it wasn't until he gave a benefit lecture in Elmira and stayed at the Langdons' house that he put the finishing touches on his courtship. Livy said yes.

Nevertheless, Livy, whose physical health had constantly worried her family, was not to be married to "the wild humorist of the Pacific Slope" without her father first checking with Sam's friends out West to find out what he was really like. Twain, meanwhile, continued his lecture tour in the East. He began to carry on a correspondence with Livy about literature, religion, and philosophy, begging her to educate and improve him. Livy saved nearly two hundred of these letters.

Finally, her father, Jervis Langdon, received the letters of reference from Sam's friends. He then asked Sam to meet privately with him.

"What kind of people are these?" Jervis Langdon asked, pointing to the letters, which had revealed Sam's worst faults. "Haven't you a friend in the world?"

"Apparently not," gulped Sam.

Then Mr. Langdon surprised Sam by concluding, "I'll be your friend, myself. Take the girl. I know you better than they do."

Once again, Twain set out on a lecture tour, and a year of waiting began for Livy. In May, proofs of *The Innocents Abroad* came from his publisher to be checked. Twain took the proofs with him to Elmira and spent happy hours with Livy, reading the proofs with her and making plans for their future. He discovered that she had a fine gift for editing, even though her spelling was terrible.

Twain saw that Livy could help him transform his writing—some of which he knew was fairly crude—into a more literary style that would find acceptance with a wider audience. More readers meant more sales.

Lecturing paid well, but Twain thought that after he was married he would prefer to stay in one place and write for newspapers or magazines. His rich future father-in-law, wishing to make life as easy as possible for his daughter, advanced Sam money to buy an interest in the *Buffalo Express*. In Buffalo, New York, Olivia would not be too far from her doting family, and Sam could resume work as a newspaperman and share the profits of ownership as well.

After completing a grueling lecture tour with forty-five stops from November through January, Twain appeared in Elmira to wed his bride on February 2, 1870. His pockets were well lined with money, some of it his payments for the phenomenal sales of *The Innocents Abroad*. He was not just a humorist anymore—he was a best-selling author.

Mr. and Mrs. Samuel L. Clemens were married in the Langdons' parlor by Joseph Twichell, who came from Hartford for the occasion, and by the Reverend Thomas Beecher, who was the Langdon family's minister in Elmira.

The next day, the bridal couple and all the guests boarded a private train car for Buffalo. Sam had asked friends to rent rooms for him while he and Livy looked for a house. A sleigh met them at the station. They were driven around and around through the snow, seemingly lost. At last the sleigh pulled up in front of a grand house on Buffalo's finest street.

"Oh, this won't do," Sam said. "People who can afford to live in this sort of style won't take boarders."

When the door opened, there stood all the wedding guests, welcoming Sam and Livy to their new home. The richly decorated house was ablaze with lights.

Sam didn't know what to say. "Don't you understand, Youth?" Livy asked, using her pet name for him. "It is ours, all ours—everything—a gift from father." The gift included the services of a cook and a housemaid, as well as a horse and carriage. Livy's father had also hired a coachman, Patrick McAleer. Livy, of course, had been in on all the planning.

From that moment on, Mark Twain relied upon Livy's organizational skills. It was Livy who arranged the domestic comforts and pleasures that surrounded them. And, many times, it was her family's money that paid for them.

The first few months in Buffalo were honeymoon-perfect. But in the spring, Jervis Langdon, Livy's beloved father, was diagnosed with cancer. He declined rapidly and died in August. Livy, who was pregnant, had a nervous collapse and could sleep only when sedated. Sam gave her constant care. He had expected to be writing a book about his frontier experiences, but for the present, writing was impossible.

Their troubles multiplied. In September a girlhood friend of Livy's came to help care for her. The friend fell ill and died of typhoid fever a month later, in Sam and Livy's bedroom, which had been converted into a sickroom.

Then in October, Livy almost miscarried. A month later, she gave birth to a weak, premature son they named Langdon. The baby was probably harmed by medications given to his mother during pregnancy. But with careful nursing he clung to life, as his father had done many years earlier in Missouri. When Langdon was only three months old, Livy caught typhoid fever and nearly died.

The stress of those months took a heavy toll on Sam Clemens. He grew to hate Buffalo. When the terrible winter of 1871 ended, he and Livy made the decision to leave. They put their house and the newspaper interest up for sale and went to spend the summer with Livy's sister Susan Crane at Quarry Farm near Elmira. There, Livy and the baby were nursed by Susan and her household.

Then Sam and Livy made a crucial decision. They would move to Hartford, where Twain's publisher, Elisha Bliss, and his new friend Joseph Twichell both lived. Livy also had friends there whose grand houses were in a parklike neighborhood called Nook Farm. She knew one of the houses was for rent and would suit them perfectly until they could build their own. Their neighbors would be the literary and cultural leaders of Hartford—people like Charles Dudley Warner, editor of the *Hartford Courant;* the family of William Gillette, the actor; Harriet Beecher Stowe, the author of *Uncle Tom's Cabin;* and other members of the famous Beecher family.

With the move to Hartford, Mark Twain found what the poet William Wordsworth had discovered: his writing drew power from "emotion recollected in tranquillity." The domestic stability of life in his grand house among family and friends would give him the power to tap childhood memories and to write his most important books.

THE HANDSOMEST TOWN

"Hartford," Mark Twain said, "is the best built and handsomest town I have ever seen.... They have the broadest, straightest streets... that ever led a sinner to destruction." He was impressed by Hartford's wealth and economic power, embodied by the insurance companies, subscription publishing houses, and the Colt firearms factory.

Hartford's location, halfway between New York City and Boston, gave Twain easy access to both cities, but Hartford didn't have the crowded feeling of either. Instead, it had a well-planned network of city streets that spread from the wooded banks of the Connecticut

River toward fields and orchards and hills. Twain felt he could be comfortable with the people he met in Hartford. They seemed more relaxed about their wealth than New Yorkers and less self-conscious about their culture than Bostonians.

Sam, who had grown up in the rural South at the edge of the frontier, had often felt like an awkward outsider in the East. But in Hartford, since Mark Twain was a popular author and he had Livy to guide him, he began to feel at home. Livy's warm, generous nature made her a favorite among their neighbors. She fit right in with the other women in the Nook Farm neighborhood, some of whom she had known for years. Livy read widely and participated in women's study and literary groups. She championed voting rights for women, dress reform, and temperance (avoiding liquor). Gently and lovingly, she led the way for her "Youth" to accept new ideas and become more refined in his behavior.

During the fall, Livy dealt with the household move, a staff of servants, the sickly baby Langdon, and another pregnancy. Twain polished the book about his frontier experiences—*Roughing It*—for publication.

In the spring of 1872, Sam and Livy went to Elmira for the birth of their second child. A healthy girl they named Olivia Susan, and always called Susy, arrived on March 19. Their joy was tempered, however, by worry over little Langdon. Three months later, when the sickly boy died of diphtheria, Sam felt a terrible guilt, saying it had been his fault for letting the child get chilled during a carriage ride.

At the end of the summer in Elmira, Livy returned to her good friends in Hartford. But Twain needed to find material for another book to keep his income flowing. The popularity of *The Innocents Abroad* and *Roughing It* convinced him he should try a similar travel book about England. In August he sailed alone to England to gather material. He was away for three months.

Everybody in England, it seemed, had heard of Mark Twain and was reading his books. He was so flattered by the attention paid him by all levels of society— invitations to banquets and country-house weekends; visits from aristocrats, authors, and actors; reporters quoting every word he spoke in public—that he couldn't write the book he had planned. It simply wouldn't do to make fun of the wonderful English people and traditions in the way that had made his other travel books so popular.

When he returned to the United States, he wrote instead a book that satirized contemporary American culture and morality. The book was called *The Gilded Age,* and Twain's coauthor was his neighbor Charles Dudley Warner, editor of the *Hartford Courant.* Twain drew on his own family's attempts to get rich and his mother's stories of her family's lost English titles and fortunes.

In early 1873, Sam and Livy bought a building lot in

Nook Farm. It was wooded and sloped down to the meandering Park River on one side and to a main Hartford avenue on another. They hired the fashionable architect Edward Tuckerman Potter to design a house worthy of their social standing.

While Livy worked on sketches and ideas to give the architect, Twain ignored most of the planning and continued his lecture tours and business ventures. Then, just as the builder brought in a crew to begin construction, the Clemens entourage—Sam, Livy, baby Susy, and several servants—left Hartford to spend nearly six months in Europe. Sam never could stand what he called the "details" of building and repair, referring half-seriously to the workers as scoundrels, idiots, and wildcats! By the time they returned, the house was nearly finished.

Livy was pregnant again. She wanted to give birth in Elmira, where she could be cared for by the female doctor who had delivered her other children and by her sister and mother. The Clemenses welcomed another robust baby girl in June 1874. They named her Clara.

TOM SAWYER

That summer, in the peaceful setting of Quarry Farm, far from lecture tours and business ventures, Mark Twain sat in the isolated comfort of a study built just for him by his sister-in-law Susan Crane. It was a small eight-sided building with windows opening on a panorama of hills and valleys and the Chemung River. There, his thoughts turned to the Missouri of his childhood.

All day, Twain worked in his study. It was his pilot-house, his private kingdom, his center of tranquillity in which to remember and savor memories of his Missouri boyhood.

The memories came flooding back to him. He gave the town of Hannibal the fictional name of St. Petersburg. His mother inspired Aunt Polly. His long-dead brother Henry was transformed into the priggish Sid. The unwashed, unschooled Tom Blankenship became the model for Huck Finn. And above all, he—the

Tom Sawyer happily loafs as a gullible friend paints the fence for him. This 1898 illustration is by J. G. Brown.

young Sam Clemens—was Tom Sawyer, with his band of friends playing pirates and Robin Hood, digging for treasure, and camping out on islands in the river. He recalled his school days and his first girlfriend, Laura Hawkins, who became Becky Thatcher. And when Tom Sawyer and Becky got lost in the cave, it wasn't far from the truth of what had really happened to Sam and Laura. In his story, though, he invented a murderer named Injun Joe to give the book its rousing climax.

Day after day, Twain wrote from the wellspring of his memory, sometimes fifty pages at a time. He began right after a hearty breakfast of steak and coffee, and he stopped around five o'clock when he returned to the main house for supper.

Filled with energy after a day's creative work, Sam joined his family, craving and receiving much loving attention. He read aloud what he had written that day and listened eagerly to Livy's suggestions for improving it.

By summer's end, the mansion in Hartford was ready to be occupied. The Clemenses moved in, with their coachman, housemaids, cook, and gardener to make them comfortable. For Sam, who had just spent the summer reminiscing about his Missouri boyhood, where his home had been a very simple wooden house, this was a dramatic contrast indeed.

No one could describe the new house without using such adjectives as "palatial," "theatrical," or simply

TOM AND HUCK

Shortly Tom came upon the juvenile pariah of the village, Huckleberry Finn, son of the town drunkard. Huckleberry was cordially hated and dreaded by all the mothers of the town, because he was idle and lawless and vulgar and bad—and because all their children admired him so, and delighted in his forbidden society, and wished they dared to be like him. Tom was like the rest of the respectable boys, in that he envied Huckleberry his gaudy outcast condition, and was under strict orders not to play with him. So he played with him every time he got a chance. . . .

Huckleberry came and went, at his own free will. He slept on doorsteps in fine weather and in empty hogsheads in wet; he did not have to go to school or to church, or call any being master or obey anybody; he could go fishing or swimming when and where he chose, and stay as long as it suited him . . . he never had to wash, nor put on clean clothes; he could swear wonderfully. In a word, everything that goes to make life precious, that boy had. So thought every harassed, hampered, respectable boy in St. Petersburg.

Tom hailed the romantic outcast:

"Hello, Huckleberry!"

"Hello yourself, and see how you like it."

"What's that you got?"

"Dead cat."

"Lemme see him Huck. My, he's pretty stiff. Where'd you get him?"

"Bought him off'n a boy."

"What did you give?"

"I give a blue ticket and a bladder that I got at the slaughter house."

"Where'd you get the blue ticket?"

"Bought it off'n Ben Rogers two weeks ago for a hoop-stick."

"Say—what is dead cats good for, Huck?"

"Good for? Cure warts with."

from *The Adventures of Tom Sawyer*

"odd." It was built in the picturesque style, in which, Twain wrote, "the house and the barn do not seem to have been set up on the grassy slopes and levels by laws and plans and specifications—it seems as if they *grew up* out of the ground and were a part and parcel of Nature's handiwork." The red brick walls, rising from a massive brownstone base, were inlaid with

The Clemens family lived happily in their grand house in Hartford, Connecticut, from 1874 to 1891. Built in large part with Olivia's inherited fortune, the house became a place of lavish entertaining.

bands of shiny black and red-orange painted bricks. Three colors of slate tiles made a diamond pattern in the roof. A variety of fancy chimneys, turrets, porches, and balconies projected from the house's top and sides. These were embellished with carved woodwork and brackets.

The nineteen-room house was ornately furnished in the best Victorian tradition. But it also held something far more valuable for the people who entered. The Clemens family radiated happiness and hospitality. Their doors were never locked, and guests were never turned away. At Christmastime, Livy always adorned the house with elaborate decorations to welcome those who stopped by.

Sam Clemens, who had grown up in poverty, had taken on the persona of Mark Twain, famous author and entertainer. The boy who had never seen a display of affection in his family had become a young father, sharing embraces with his wife and daughters. The rough Westerner with only a grade-school education was an honored member of the literary and cultural elite of the East Coast. Sam Clemens had finally found his fortune, and if it wasn't solid gold, it was at least gilded.

Mark Twain wrote much of his best work, including The Adventures of Tom Sawyer, at this table in his study at Elmira, New York.

Chapter **SIX**

THE
HOUSEHOLD
HIVE

IN THE FALL OF 1874, TWAIN'S FRIEND WILLIAM Dean Howells, who was editor of the *Atlantic Monthly,* asked him to write a series of articles for the prestigious magazine. Twain agreed, then panicked when he couldn't think of a subject. On a long walk with Joseph Twichell in the brilliant autumn woods, Twain began to reminisce about the days when he piloted a steamboat on the Mississippi. Twichell listened enthralled, and when the walk was over said, "What a virgin subject to hurl into a magazine!"

Twain hadn't thought of that before, but the memories came swiftly, and within ten days he had finished three articles for the magazine. The articles portrayed life on the river and the kaleidoscope of characters he had met. Enriching the stories was a style of writing that reflected the river itself, its ebb and flow, its snags and safe channels.

The Clemens family returned to Elmira for the summer of 1875, and it was there that Twain again found peace and quiet. He finished writing *The Adventures of Tom Sawyer*. It was finally published in June 1876.

Twain decided to write a sequel to *Tom Sawyer*, and he used the boy named Huckleberry Finn as the narrator. Twain had seen Hartford children gathering buckets of huckleberries—until then, he said, he thought huckleberries were something like turnips. "I never saw any place where morality and huckleberries flourished as they do here," he wrote of Hartford.

In *The Adventures of Tom Sawyer*, Tom's friend Huck Finn had been patterned on Twain's own boyhood friend, Tom Blankenship. The Blankenship family provided him with more characters and ideas for his new story. Tom's violent father—combined with Jimmy Finn, the town drunk—became Pap Finn. And the episode of a boy hiding a runaway slave was based on Tom Blankenship's older brother's adventure helping a slave escape.

Jim, the other main character in the book, was inspired by Uncle Dan'l, Twain's faithful childhood friend on his uncle's farm. As Twain wrote, "It was on the farm that I got my strong liking for his race and my appreciation of certain of its fine qualities. . . . This feeling and this estimate have stood the test of [many

Huck and Jim

Mark Twain had an ear for the perfect pitch of America's regional speech. To hear what Twain heard, it is important to read these passages slowly, and preferably aloud. Here, Huck and Jim are on the raft with two con men who say they're a king and a duke:

By and by, when they was asleep and snoring, Jim says:
"Don't it s'prise you, de way dem kings carries on, Huck?"
"No," I says, "it don't."
"Why don't it, Huck?"
"Well, it don't, because it's in the breed. I reckon they're all alike."
"But, Huck, dese kings o' ourn is reglar rapscallions; dat's jist what dey is; dey's reglar rapscallions."
"Well, that's what I'm a-saying; all kings is mostly rapscallions, as fur as I can make out."
"Is dat so?"
"You read about them once—you'll see. Look at Henry the Eight; this'n 's a Sunday-school Superintendent to HIM. . . . My, you ought to seen old Henry the Eight when he was in bloom. He WAS a blossom. He used to marry a new wife every day, and chop off her head next morning. And he would do it just as indifferent as if he was ordering up eggs. 'Fetch up Nell Gwynn,' he says. They fetch her up. Next morning, 'Chop off her head!' And they chop it off. . . . And he made every one of them tell him a tale every night; and he kept that up till he had hogged a thousand and one tales that way. . . . You don't know kings, Jim, but I know them; and this old rip of ourn is one of the cleanest I've struck in history. . . ."
"But dis one do smell so like de nation, Huck."
"Well, they all do, Jim. We can't help the way a king smells; history don't tell no way."

from *Adventures of Huckleberry Finn*

years] and have suffered no impairment. The black face is as welcome to me now as it was then."

Twain remembered the way Uncle Dan'l spoke, and his speech patterns rolled from Jim's mouth. Twain's "perfect pitch for the American vernacular [speech patterns]" was at the heart of his genius as a writer.

John T. Lewis, a tenant farmer at Quarry Farm, and George Griffin, the Clemens's long-time butler in Hartford, also contributed to the character of Jim. Twain had a great affection for these black men, resulting in his noblest fictional character—the man whom Huck helps to free.

Twain wrote swiftly, and by the end of the summer he had finished the first sixteen chapters. Then suddenly, his inspiration stopped. "I made the great discovery that when the tank runs dry you've only to leave it alone and it will fill up again in time," he wrote. "While you are asleep—also while you are at work at other things and are quite unaware that this . . . is going on."

He turned his attention to other matters. He and a friend from Western days wrote and produced a play that closed after only a week on a New York stage. He wrote a few magazine articles and outlined another novel. At the end of the year, he gave a speech in Boston to honor the poet John Greenleaf Whittier on his seventieth birthday. It was a disaster. It was crude, and it embarrassed the audience of eminent literary men. Twain felt humiliated.

His publisher was asking for another book, but Twain's tank was dry. In April 1878, he took his family to Europe again, this time for a sixteen-month stay in which he planned to lecture, write, and renew himself.

During his extended stay in Europe, Twain and his friend Joseph Twichell went on a month-long tour in Switzerland and Germany. Twain based a travel book, *A Tramp Abroad,* on the tour and a character in the book, Mr. Harris, on Twichell.

The Clemens family returned to the United States in the fall of 1879. The next July, they were in Elmira when their third daughter was born. She was officially named Jane Lampton after Sam's mother, but they called her Jean.

Another addition to the family that summer was twenty-four-year-old Katy Leary. She served the Clemenses as nanny, seamstress, nurse, traveling companion, and personal maid to Olivia. Many members of the household staff stayed with the Clemenses for years. Patrick McAleer, the coachman, had started working for them right after their wedding. The butler, George Griffin, was a former slave who came, Twain said, to wash windows and stayed for eighteen years. George and Patrick doted on the Clemens girls and were both protectors and playmates. Patrick once told Clara—who longed for a pony—that if she combed their calf every day, it would turn into a horse. Alas, one day she discovered horns growing from the calf's head, and the game was up!

In 1880 Twain began work on a novel set in medieval England—a romantic tale of a young prince and a poor boy who looked alike and traded places. It was called *The Prince and the Pauper*. In some ways, the boys were medieval versions of Tom Sawyer and Huck Finn. Twain addressed many of his favorite themes—twins, oppression, and social injustice—with both satire and humor. Livy, eight-year-old Susy, and six-year-old Clara told him it was the best writing he had ever done.

Sam made up stories for his daughters every night. Often they insisted on a romance that included mention of the dozen or more bric-á-brac displayed on the mantelpiece and the bookshelves next to it. Each story had to be different. He couldn't leave out a single object. And he always had to begin at one end with the picture of a cat wearing an Elizabethan ruff around its neck and continue through vases and figurines to the painting of a young girl they called "Emmeline" at the other. "In the course of time," Sam said, "the bric-á-brac and the pictures showed wear. It was because they had had so many and such tumultuous adventures in their romantic careers."

Twain loved to play charades and dress up in costumes. "Clothes make the man," he joked. "Naked people have little or no influence in society."

He found a great playmate in Joseph Twichell. The two men tried riding newfangled high-wheeled bicycles and wobbled off together down the Hartford

A radiant Clemens family sat for their portrait on the porch of their Hartford home in 1884. From left to right: *Clara, Livy, Jean, Sam, and Susy. The dog's name is Hash.*

street, laughing like boys and falling off. "Mr. Clemens," said their young instructor, "it's remarkable—you can fall off of a bicycle more different ways than the man that invented it."

LIFE IN THE GRAND HOUSE

Life in the grand house grew ever more lavish. Famous visitors from many countries came—and stayed and stayed—captivated by the Clemenses' warm hospitality and opulent lifestyle. Livy finally begged her gregarious husband not to invite everyone he met to visit him in Hartford, because they always came.

The dinner parties, with spectacular menus of oysters, duck, roast beef, champagne and claret, ice cream molds, and chestnut pudding provided a chance for Mark Twain to perform. Between courses, he walked around the table, waving his napkin and regaling guests with stories. He often entertained them on the piano afterward. He sang spirituals in his

A costumed Mark Twain and his daughter Susy entertained fellow guests at the Onteora Club, a literary colony in New York's Catskill Mountains.

warm tenor voice and moved them to laughter—or tears. After the guests had left, Livy sometimes pointed out to her Youth the defects or excesses of his performance—in what their daughters called "dusting off papa."

After dinner parties and on Friday nights, he and his friends climbed to the third-floor billiard room. They turned the air hazy with cigar smoke and shot balls around the kittens that often played on the table or grabbed at the balls from pockets.

Twain found it almost impossible to do any steady writing in what he termed the "household hive." Susy, "the busiest bee," and Clara learned their lessons from tutors at home. At the age of two, Jean caught scarlet fever. Suddenly, her health became a serious worry for her parents.

The worry about Jean, the older girls' constant activities, and his need to conduct his own business affairs wreaked havoc on Twain's concentration. He tried working in a room in his carriage house. Then he went up the street to the Twichells' house. Finally, he moved his desk and his chaos of papers to the third-floor billiard room. There he tried to write, but often took out his frustrations on Katy Leary, accusing her of throwing away valuable papers when she dusted. Small wonder, then, that it was during the summers at Quarry Farm in Elmira, in the more peaceful isolation of his octagonal study, that Twain did most of his sustained book writing.

Sam felt continuous pressure to bring in more money as expenses spiraled. From the time he was a printer's apprentice, he had been fascinated by any invention that would speed up the process of setting type. Now he hoped to profit by speculating on some innovative machinery for the printing industry. He sank money into a doomed engraving process called the Kaolotype. He also began to feed large quantities of money to the hungriest speculation of all: the compositor for automatic typesetting that James W. Paige was building at the Colt firearms factory.

HOME TO HANNIBAL

In the spring of 1882, desperately needing renewal and inspiration for his writing, Twain spent six weeks traveling along the Mississippi River. He went to see Hannibal for the first time in fifteen years. Upon seeing it again, it seemed that "everything was changed in Hannibal—but when I reached Third or Fourth street the tears burst forth, for I recognized the mud."

The material he gathered gave him enough subject matter and creative inspiration to "fill up his tank." He wrote *Life on the Mississippi,* and seven years after he began, he was able to finish writing *Adventures of Huckleberry Finn.* "I haven't had such booming working-days for many years," he wrote joyfully to his mother and Orion. Twain acknowledged that these sudden and periodic changes of mood, from joyful productivity to "deep melancholy to half-insane tempests and cyclones of humor, are among the curiosities of my life."

Hoping to increase his profits from writing by becoming his own publisher, Twain established a publishing house. He put his nephew, Pamela's son-in-law Charles Webster, in charge of it and named it for him. *Adventures of Huckleberry Finn*, published in 1885, was the company's first book.

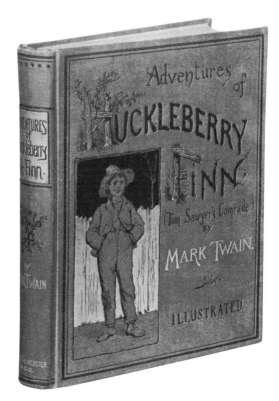

The first edition of Adventures of Huckleberry Finn *introduced a slouching, straw-hatted Huck, drawn by E. W. Kemble.*

Twain arranged another long speaking tour and invited the southern novelist George Washington Cable to share the platform and provide companionship. Twain had designed a new kind of program, an author's reading based on the style of Charles Dickens's performances, in which he and Cable read from and acted out their stories. The "Twins of Genius" gave 104 performances, traveled 10,000 miles, and stayed in hotel rooms in 70 cities. Before it ended, Twain grew miserably homesick, feuded with Cable, and ranted against being expected "to paint himself striped and stand on his head every fifteen minutes."

Audiences loved the readings by Mark Twain and George Washington Cable. But after four months of touring with him, Twain called Cable a pious bore who taught him to hate all religions and abhor the Sabbath day!

In spite of his ravings, Twain had perfected a fool-proof platform style that earned him a lot of money quickly. "Ah, well," he wrote to a friend, "I am a great & sublime fool. But then I am God's fool, & all His works must be contemplated with respect."

One person who contemplated Twain with respect was his eldest daughter, Susy. In 1885, at the age of thirteen, Susy began to write a biography of her father. Twain was almost fifty. Her youthful honesty—and misspellings—flattered and delighted him. "He is a very good man," Susy wrote, "and a very funny one; he has got a temper, but we all have in this family. He is the loveliest man I ever saw, or ever hope to see." Twain often quoted from Susy's biography and then added his own version of the events she related.

Early reviews of *Huckleberry Finn* were not all positive. Twain was hurt and angered by accusations that the book's bad grammar, low morality, and coarseness made it suitable only for the slums. The Concord Free Public Library in Massachusetts, citing these complaints, became the first in a long list of libraries and schools to banish the book from its shelves.

Twain's next book was *A Connecticut Yankee in King Arthur's Court,* published in 1889. It was a science fiction story about a Hartford mechanic working at the Colt firearms factory who is struck on the head with a crowbar and wakes up in King Arthur's England. The public didn't quite know what to make of the book—a curious mixture of humor and social criticism, medieval warfare and modern technology. American readers were generally amused. British readers, on the other hand, expected another typical children's story of switched identities, like those popular at the time. But what they found was a savage attack on their honored traditions of monarchy, the privileged classes, and the established Church of England.

When Twain visited England seventeen years earlier, in 1872, he had been flattered by the attention given to him by these very people and institutions. But as the years passed, he became increasingly opposed to any institutions he considered to be antidemocratic or oppressive. In *A Connecticut Yankee,* he gave vent to his anger.

That same year, nine-year-old Jean began having epileptic seizures. Her desperate parents tried to find cures even as they kept her condition carefully hidden from outsiders.

The next year, in 1890, Susy left home to enter Bryn Mawr College in Pennsylvania. It was a heartbreaking departure for both father and daughter, and Sam found as many excuses as he could to visit Susy at school.

That autumn, both Sam's mother and Livy's mother died. Their deaths further diminished the family. About the same time, Livy was diagnosed with heart disease. Sam himself developed such debilitating pain in his right arm that he had to teach himself to write left-handed or stop writing altogether.

By June 1891, Sam's financial situation had reached a crisis. There was only one thing to do to stop the constant outflow of money as the Clemens family hosted guest after guest. He and Livy closed the costly Hartford house and took the family to Europe, where they could save money by living in rented houses or hotels.

Livy could scarcely bear to leave her beloved house with all its wonderful memories. The carriage arrived to take them to the station, but she went back into the house, walking from room to room, saying a silent good-bye to the home she might never see again.

Sam also felt the moment deeply. "To us, our house was not unsentient matter," he wrote to his friend Joseph Twichell. "It had a heart, and a soul, and eyes to see us with; and approvals, and solicitudes, and deep sympathies; it was of us, and we were in its confidence, and lived in its grace and in the peace of its benediction. . . . We could not enter it unmoved."

A vigorous Mark Twain, photographed here in 1894, overcame bankruptcy and personal tragedies and became America's first modern celebrity.

Chapter SEVEN

MAN IN THE WHITE SUIT

SAM AND LIVY TOOK ELEVEN-YEAR-OLD JEAN WITH them to Aix-les-Bains, France, where they hoped the sulfur baths would improve their health. Livy's sister Susan Crane was with them and so was Katy Leary, who packed and unpacked the twenty-five trunks they carried. Nineteen-year-old Susy and seventeen-year-old Clara went to Switzerland to study French, then the whole family reunited for winter in Berlin, Germany.

Mark Twain was so famous that he was recognized wherever he went. Even Kaiser Wilhelm II was a fan. When the German ruler invited Twain to dinner, Jean was astounded. "Why, papa," she said, "if it keeps on going like this, pretty soon there won't be anybody left for you to get acquainted with but God."

The family moved on to Florence, Italy. There, Twain began work on a novel about Joan of Arc, whom he had idealized since the day long ago when a page of her history blew in front of him on a Hannibal street. His fictionalized Joan of Arc, who was inspired by his daughter Susy, behaved like a feminist of the late 1800s.

During the next two years, Twain made four transatlantic trips back to the United States to take care of his rapidly declining business affairs. He was advised—rescued, more accurately—by the financier

Mark Twain moved his family to Europe in 1891 to cut expenses. Here, he and Susy are on board the SS La Gascogne.

Henry H. Rogers of Standard Oil, who admired Twain and offered free counsel. The stock market crashed in 1893, and the economic crisis that followed destroyed Twain's business investments. In 1894, when Rogers advised Twain to abandon his publishing house and the Paige Compositor and to declare bankruptcy, Twain knew it was the only possible way to get out of debt.

Sam and Livy were determined to pay back their creditors dollar for dollar, even though half that would have fulfilled their legal obligation. Sam was fifty-nine years old, and Livy was not well, but they decided to go around the world on a lecture tour and use the earnings to pay the debt. Clara would go with them.

Before beginning the exhausting tour, the family gathered for a happy summer in Elmira. At the end of the summer, Sam, Livy, and Clara said good-bye to Susy and Jean, who wanted to stay with their Aunt Susan and Katy Leary in Elmira. Susy went with them to the train station and stood on the platform waving until the train was out of sight.

Beginning in Cleveland, Twain gave his readings to full-capacity audiences all the way to the West Coast. He thoroughly enjoyed himself. Livy, too, seemed to thrive. In September they sailed for Australia, then on to perform in New Zealand, Ceylon, India, and South Africa. Nearly a year later, in July 1896, he was truly the toast of several continents when he arrived triumphantly in England with most of his debts paid.

THUNDER-STROKES

Susy, Jean, and Katy Leary planned to join Sam, Livy, and Clara in England in mid-August. But on the day they were expected, Sam and Livy received a letter stating that Susy had fallen ill while visiting the Warners in Hartford. Transatlantic cables followed, and then, with a premonition that all was not well, Livy and Clara sailed for America. They were still at sea, and Sam was alone, when another cable was handed to him three days later.

"Susy was peacefully released today," it said simply. At the age of twenty-four, Susy had died of spinal meningitis—in their own beloved Hartford house, where she had asked the Warners to carry her during her final days. Katy Leary was with her.

"It is one of the mysteries of our nature that a man, all unprepared, can receive a thunder-stroke like that and live," Sam wrote.

Sam and Livy's grief far outweighed any they felt before or after. They were devastated. It took nearly two years before the darkness lifted. During that time, Sam wrote compulsively just to keep his sanity. Livy hung on for her Youth's sake, even as her own health continued to weaken.

The family spent much of that time in Austria, mostly Vienna, where Twain again found himself the focus of an adoring public. Their hotel suites attracted gatherings of rich, famous, and merely curious visitors from the worlds of art, politics, and aristocracy.

Mark Twain was recognized everywhere and consulted by newspaper reporters on every subject. He became the toast of Vienna.

Twain turned the story of his remarkable round-the-world lecture tour into a travel book, *Following the Equator*. The excitement and surprise of discovery that marked Twain's earlier travel books had worn off. Even so, there were enough of Twain's unique touches to charm his readers. His humor was less forced and his observations more gentle and thoughtful: "In New Zealand the rabbit plague began at Bluff. The man who introduced the rabbit there was banqueted and lauded; but they would hang him, now, if they could get him. In England the natural enemy of the rabbit is detested and persecuted; in the Bluff region the natural enemy of the rabbit is honored, and his person is sacred. . . . In England any person below the Heir who is caught with a rabbit in his possession must satisfactorily explain how it got there, or he will suffer fine and imprisonment. . . . All governments are more or less short-sighted: in England they fine the poacher, whereas he ought to be banished to New Zealand. New Zealand would pay his way, and give him wages."

With his debts paid by March 1898 and payments continuing to pour in from his books, Twain regained his old spirit. His long exile from America was nearly over. In October 1900, he returned with Livy, twenty-seven-year-old Clara, and twenty-one-year-old Jean to a hero's welcome in New York. The adulation of

Americans for their most honored man of letters continued. Twain's books captured a worldwide audience. Sales of his books soared. He was called "sole, incomparable, the Lincoln of our literature."

Mark Twain, always the one to say it best, remarked, "My books are water; those of the great geniuses are wine. Everybody drinks water."

Hartford had changed in the decade that Sam and Livy had been absent. Many of their friends had died or moved away, and there were tragic reminders of Susy there. So the Clemens family settled in New York City, where many of their circle of friends, financial advisers, and publishers lived. They stayed there until Livy's health became so poor that her doctors recommended the family move back to Italy's mild climate.

After a steady decline, Livy died in Florence in 1904. Although Sam ached with loneliness, he was comforted by the realization that Livy's death had spared her more suffering. Jean once more began to have seizures, and Clara had a nervous breakdown. Twain sadly returned to the United States to live in a house on lower Fifth Avenue in New York City.

FINAL HARVEST

In 1905 Mark Twain turned seventy, and his publishers invited two hundred guests to a banquet in his honor at Delmonico's Restaurant in New York City. It was a celebrity night of the highest order, with music by a forty-piece orchestra, champagne and brandy flowing, and five hours of tributes to Twain from the distinguished company.

Two years later, an even greater honor brought world attention to Mark Twain when he was awarded a doctor of letters degree by Oxford University in England. Splendidly dressed in his scarlet and gray robe, he was welcomed with a tumult of shouts from the undergraduates as he stood to receive the honor. Afterward, he was surrounded by cheering crowds and escorted through the streets.

Mark Twain said he would have been willing to journey to Mars for the honorary doctorate he received from England's Oxford University in 1907.

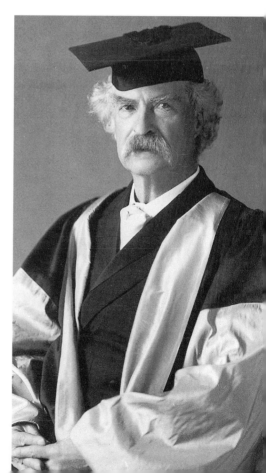

Mark Twain was so famous that he outshone the thirty other men who were also given honorary degrees that day. These included his friend and fellow author Rudyard Kipling, the composer Camille Saint-Saëns, the sculptor Auguste Rodin, King Edward VII's brother Prince Arthur, and the Prime Minister of England! It seemed that the people had eyes only for Mark Twain, who was "the most advertised man in the world," according to *Harper's Weekly*. The boy from Hannibal, long years after hearing his mother's stories of the family's lost titles and fortunes, had claimed new ones for himself.

Back in New York, Mark Twain began wearing white serge suits year-round, to the embarrassment of his daughters and the amusement of friends. He called them his "don't-care-a-damn suits." On Sundays he waited in the lobby of the Plaza Hotel until church services ended. Then he strolled down Fifth Avenue in his white suit, loving the attention he got from fashionable strangers, who tipped their hats to him. He had magically transferred his stage personality onto the very streets he walked and had become America's first modern celebrity.

He also dressed up in the brilliant Oxford robe on any pretext, including for Clara's wedding!

It seemed that everyone important wanted to have Mark Twain on their guest list. He was worn out by the many dinners in his honor. He finally decided to arrive right in time for the after-dinner speeches and

Flaunting his Oxford robes, Mark Twain posed with Clara on the day of her wedding to Ossip Gabrilowitsch in 1909. From left to right: *Twain, nephew Jervis Langdon, daughter Jean, Ossip, Clara, and the Reverend Joseph Twichell.*

forego the rich food. This glut of food reminded him of the sumptuous feasts of his childhood at the Quarles farm in Missouri, and he talked about those feasts while dictating his autobiography.

He built a new mansion for himself in Redding, Connecticut, and called it Stormfield. There, Twain tried to reproduce the same elegance of living and entertaining that he had known in Hartford. But he was increasingly lonely. He grieved for Livy and Susy,

Clara lived in Europe, Jean was in and out of sanatoriums for her health, and Joseph Twichell no longer lived close enough to comfort him.

Twain stopped writing of boyhood nostalgia and travel experiences. Instead, he explored a darker and more troubled world in works such as *The Diaries of Adam and Eve, What Is Man?,* and *Extract from Captain Stormfield's Visit to Heaven.*

His health began to fail. Doctors diagnosed Twain's chest pains as angina pectoris, a heart condition. But he continued with his marathon cigar smoking and social life in spite of it. He hired a young writer, Albert Bigelow Paine, to take dictation for his autobiography.

Sam returned from a vacation in Bermuda in December 1909 to spend Christmas at Stormfield. Clara had married the musician Ossip Gabrilowitsch earlier in the year and was abroad. Jean was there—home at last after long stays in sanatoriums. She busily wrapped gifts and decorated the house as elaborately as her mother had done in Hartford. On Christmas Eve, Sam kissed his daughter good night and went to his bedroom. Early Christmas morning, Sam was wakened by a frantic Katy Leary. Jean was dead! She had probably died of a heart attack brought on by an epileptic seizure.

Sam did not have the strength to follow the hearse. He watched from the window as it carried Jean's coffin through a heavy snowstorm to the train that would take her to Elmira. She was buried next to her mother, Livy, her sister Susy, and her infant brother, Langdon.

With no family left at Stormfield, Sam sought comfort again in Bermuda. Just a few months later, in April, suffering from heart failure and not wishing to die away from home, he returned to Stormfield.

Earlier in the year, he had commented that Halley's Comet was coming again for the first time since he was born in 1835 and that he expected "to go out with it. . . . The Almighty has said, no doubt: 'Now here are these unaccountable freaks; they came in together, they must go out together.' Oh! I am looking forward to that."

As the sun set on April 21, 1910, Mark Twain died. Halley's Comet had just passed the point in its orbit nearest the sun and was lighting out for uncharted territory.

SOURCES

8   Albert Bigelow Paine, *Mark Twain, a Biography* (New York: Harper & Brothers, 1912), 1:76.

8   Albert Bigelow Paine, ed., *Mark Twain's Autobiography* (New York: Harper & Brothers, 1924), 2:282.

9   Mark Twain, *Chapters from My Autobiography* (New York: Harper & Brothers, 1906), 9:6.

14 Ibid., 13:459.

15 Mark Twain, *Life on the Mississippi* (Boston: James R. Osgood, 1883), 64.

18 Dixon Wecter, *Sam Clemens of Hannibal* (Boston: Houghton Mifflin, 1952), 88.

19 Twain, *Chapters from My Autobiography*, 13:452.

20 Ibid., 13:462, 461.

21 Ibid., 13:461, 456.

21 Ibid., 5:839.

23 Twain, *Life on the Mississippi*, 62–3.

23 Paine, *Mark Twain, a Biography*, 1:65.

24 Paine, *Mark Twain's Autobiography*, 1:124.

24 Wecter, *Sam Clemens of Hannibal*, 58.

24 Twain, *Life on the Mississippi*, 44–5.

26 Ibid., 65.

27 Ibid.

27 Paine, *Mark Twain's Autobiography*, 1:308.

29 Albert Bigelow Paine, *The Adventures of Mark Twain* (New York: Grosset & Dunlap, 1944), 40.

32 Wecter, *Sam Clemens of Hannibal*, 258.

34 Mark Twain, "The Turning Point of My Life," in *Tales, Speeches, Essays, and Sketches* (New York: Penguin, 1994), 340.

35 Twain, *Life on the Mississippi*, 79.

37 Ibid., 111.

38 Ibid., 118.

46 Paine, *The Adventures of Mark Twain*, 122–3.

47 Ibid., 123.

50 *Mark Twain's Letters* (Berkeley, CA: University of California, 1988), 1:323.

51 Mark Twain, *Roughing It* (Hartford, CT: American Publishing, 1872), 534, 537.

51 Paine, *Mark Twain, a Biography*, 1:287.

55 Mark Twain, *The Innocents Abroad* (Hartford, CT: American Publishing, 1869), 287–8.

56 Charles Neider, introduction to *The Complete Short Stories of Mark Twain* (Garden City, NY: Doubleday, 1957), xv.

56 Twain, *Tales, Speeches, Essays, and Sketches*, 75.

59 Paine, *Mark Twain, a Biography*, 1:353.

61 Paine, *Mark Twain's Autobiography*, 2:110–11.

63 Justin Kaplan, *Mr. Clemens and Mark Twain* (New York: Simon & Schuster, 1966), 28.

63 Paine, *The Adventures of Mark Twain*, 181.

65 William Wordsworth, preface to "Lyrical Ballads, with Other Poems" (London: T. N. Longman and O. Rees), 1800.

65 Mark Twain, "A Glimpse of Hartford," in *Alta California*, March 3, 1868.

72 *Mark Twain's Letters*, 6.

75 Paine, *Mark Twain, a Biography*, 1:531.

76 Mark Twain, "Morality and Huckleberries," in *Alta California*, September 6, 1868.

76 Paine, *Mark Twain's Autobiography*, 1:100–1.

78 E. L. Doctorow, introduction to *The Adventures of Tom Sawyer* (New York: Oxford University Press, 1996), xxxvii.

78 Bernard deVoto, ed., *Mark Twain in Eruption* (New York: Harper & Brothers, 1922), 197.

80 Twain, *Chapters from My Autobiography*, 4:710.

80 Merle Johnson, *More Maxims of Mark*, (New York: 1927).

81 Paine, *Mark Twain, a Biography*, 1:767.

83 Paine, *Mark Twain's Autobiography*, 2:156.

83 Twain, *Chapters from My Autobiography*, 4:45.

84 Albert Bigelow Paine, ed., *Mark Twain's Notebook* (New York: Harper & Brothers, 1935), 163.

84 Albert Bigelow Paine, ed., *Mark Twain's Letters* (New York: Harper & Brothers, 1917), 1:434.

85   deVoto, *Mark Twain in Eruption*, 251.
86   Henry Nash Smith and William M. Gibson, eds., *Mark Twain–Howells Letters* (Cambridge: Harvard University Press, 1960), 1:215.
87   Ibid.
87   Twain, *Chapters from My Autobiography*, 4:709.
89   Paine, *Mark Twain's Letters*, 2:641.
91   Twain, *Chapters from My Autobiography*, 14:562.
94   Ibid., 3:580.
95   Mark Twain, *Following the Equator* (Hartford, CT: American Publishing, 1897), 285–6.
96   William Dean Howells, *My Mark Twain* (New York: Harper & Brothers, 1910), 101.
96   Paine, *Mark Twain's Notebook*, 190.
98   Kaplan, *Mr. Clemens and Mark Twain*, 382.
101 Clara Clemens, *My Father: Mark Twain* (New York: Harper & Brothers, 1931), 279.

BIBLIOGRAPHY

SELECTED WRITINGS OF MARK TWAIN

Works by Mark Twain can be found in many editions and under three different file names: Clemens, Samuel; Twain, Mark; and Mark Twain. Twain's first U.S. editions have been printed in facsimile in the twenty-nine-volume *Oxford Mark Twain*, published in 1996 by Oxford University Press.

The Celebrated Jumping Frog of Calaveras County and Other Sketches, 1867.
The Innocents Abroad, 1869.
Roughing It, 1872.
The Gilded Age, 1874.
Sketches, New and Old, 1875.
The Adventures of Tom Sawyer, 1876.

A Tramp Abroad, 1880.
The Prince and the Pauper, 1881.
The Stolen White Elephant and Other Detective Stories, 1882.
Life on the Mississippi, 1883.
Adventures of Huckleberry Finn, 1885.
A Connecticut Yankee in King Arthur's Court, 1889.
Merry Tales, 1892.
The American Claimant, 1892.
The £1,000,000 Bank-Note and Other New Stories, 1893.
Tom Sawyer Abroad, 1894.
*The Tragedy of Pudd'nhead Wilson and the Comedy, Those
    Extraordinary Twins,* 1894.
Personal Recollections of Joan of Arc, 1896.
How to Tell a Story and Other Essays, 1897.
Following the Equator, 1897.
The Man That Corrupted Hadleyburg and Other Stories and Essays,
    1900.
The Diaries of Adam and Eve, 1904, 1906.
What Is Man?, 1906.
The $30,000 Bequest and Other Stories, 1906.
Chapters from My Autobiography, 1906-1907.
Extract from Captain Stormfield's Visit to Heaven, 1909.
Speeches, 1910.

Paine, Albert Bigelow, ed. *Mark Twain's Letters.* 2 vols. New York:
    Harper & Brothers, 1917.
_____. *Mark Twain's Notebook.* New York: Harper & Brothers,
    1935.
_____. *Mark Twain's Speeches.* New York: Harper & Brothers,
    1910.
Smith, Henry Nash and William M. Gibson, eds. *Mark Twain–
    Howells Letters: The Correspondence of Samuel L. Clemens and
    William D. Howells, 1872–1910.* Cambridge: Harvard
    University Press, 1960.
Wecter, Dixon, ed. *The Love Letters of Mark Twain.* New York:
    Harper & Brothers, 1949.
_____. *Mark Twain's Letters to Mrs. Fairbanks.* San Marino, CA:
    Huntington Library, 1949.

The *Mark Twain Project,* based at the Bancroft Library of the University of California at Berkeley, is where nearly all of the manuscripts and correspondence of Mark Twain are located. The *Mark Twain Project* is an ongoing project dedicated to publishing authoritative, annotated volumes of all of Mark Twain's papers.

Mark Twain's Letters, Vols. 1–6, 1853–1875. University of
    California at Berkeley: 1988, 1990, 1992, 1995, 1997, 2001.
Mark Twain's Notebooks and Journals, Vols. 1–3, 1855–1891.
    University of California at Berkeley: 1975, 1979.

OTHER SOURCES

Andrews, Kenneth R. *Nook Farm: Mark Twain's Hartford Circle.*
    Cambridge, MA: Harvard University Press, 1950.
Ayres, Alex, ed. *The Wit & Wisdom of Mark Twain.* New York:
    Harper & Row, 1987.
Clemens, Clara. *My Father: Mark Twain.* New York: Harper &
    Brothers, 1931.
Clemens, Susy. *Papa: An Intimate Biography of Mark Twain.*
    Edited by Charles Neider. Garden City, NY: Doubleday, 1985.
Gribben, Alan, and Nick Karanovich, eds. *Overland with Mark
    Twain: James B. Pond's Photographs and Journal of the North
    American Lecture Tour of 1895.* Elmira, NY: Center for Mark
    Twain Studies at Quarry Farm, 1992.
Howells, William Dean. *My Mark Twain: Reminiscences and
    Criticisms.* New York: Harper & Brothers, 1910.
Kaplan, Justin. *Mark Twain and His World.* New York: Simon &
    Schuster, 1974.
_____. *Mr. Clemens and Mark Twain.* New York: Simon &
    Schuster, 1966.
Lawton, Mary. *A Lifetime with Mark Twain: The Memories of Katy
    Leary, for Thirty Years His Faithful and Devoted Servant.* New
    York: Harcourt Brace, 1925.
Meltzer, Milton. *Mark Twain Himself.* New York: Thomas Y.
    Crowell, 1960.

Paine, Albert Bigelow. *The Adventures of Mark Twain* (original title: *The Boys' Life of Mark Twain*, 1915). New York: Grosset & Dunlap, 1944.

_____. *Mark Twain, a Biography.* 2 vols. New York: Harper & Brothers, 1912.

Powers, Ron. *Dangerous Water, a Biography of the Boy Who Became Mark Twain.* New York: Basic Books, 1999.

Salsbury, Edith Colgate, ed. *Susy and Mark Twain: Family Dialogues.* New York: Harper & Row, 1965.

Skandera-Trombley, Laura. *Mark Twain in the Company of Women.* Philadelphia: University of Pennsylvania Press, 1994.

Wecter, Dixon. *Sam Clemens of Hannibal.* Boston: Houghton, Mifflin, 1952.

WEBSITE

<http://about.com/arts/marktwain>
This site is a treasure trove of links to banned books, a biography, criticism, homes and haunts, impersonators, manuscripts, and all sorts of other subjects, including Twain's own works and humor in the style of Mark Twain.

Birthplace: Florida, Missouri

> The house in which Mark Twain was born is inside a modern museum in Mark Twain State Park.
>
> Mark Twain Birthplace State Historical Site
> 37352 Shrine Road, Stoutsville, MO 65283-9722
> <http://www.mostateparks.com/twainsite.htm>

Boyhood Home: Hannibal, Missouri

> A historic district includes the boyhood home at 206 Hill Street, the Becky Thatcher House, Marshall Clemens's law office, and statues of Mark Twain, Tom Sawyer, and Huckleberry Finn. "Mark Twain's cave" south of town and a steamboat ride on the river are other attractions.
>
> Mark Twain's Boyhood Home and Museum
> 208 Hill Street, Hannibal, MO 63401-3316
> <http://www.artcom.com/museums/vs/mr/63401.htm>

Elmira, New York

> Mark Twain and his family spent nearly every summer for more than twenty years at Quarry Farm in Elmira, home of Olivia's sister and brother-in-law, Susan and Theodore Crane. The "octagonal study," in which Mark Twain wrote the majority of his best work, is on the campus of Elmira College. Mark Twain and his family are buried in Elmira's Woodlawn Cemetery.
>
> Center for Mark Twain Studies
> Elmira College, Elmira, NY 14902
> <http://www.elmira.edu/MarkTwain/twainhom.htm>

Mark Twain House: Hartford, Connecticut

> The house Mark Twain built and lived in from 1874 to 1891 is authentically restored to its original elegance. Twain and his family spent their happiest years in this house, enjoying a lavish lifestyle. Open for tours year-round.
>
> The Mark Twain House
> 351 Farmington Avenue, Hartford, CT 06105
> (860) 247-0998
> <http://www.hartnet.org/twain/>

INDEX

OTHER TITLES FROM LERNER AND A&E®:

Arthur Ashe
Bill Gates
Bruce Lee
Carl Sagan
Chief Crazy Horse
Christopher Reeve
Edgar Allan Poe
Eleanor Roosevelt
George Lucas
Gloria Estefan
Jack London
Jacques Cousteau
Jane Austen
Jesse Owens
Jesse Ventura
Jimi Hendrix
John Glenn
Latin Sensations

Legends of Dracula
Legends of Santa Claus
Louisa May Alcott
Madeleine Albright
Maya Angelou
Mohandas Gandhi
Mother Teresa
Nelson Mandela
Princess Diana
Queen Cleopatra
Queen Latifah
Rosie O'Donnell
Saint Joan of Arc
Thurgood Marshall
Wilma Rudolph
Women in Space
Women of the Wild West

ABOUT THE AUTHOR

Susan Bivin Aller lives with her husband in West Hartford, Connecticut, near the house Mark Twain built, and they are actively involved in programs at the house. Susan is the author of *J. M. Barrie: The Magic behind Peter Pan, Emma and the Night Dogs,* and several nonfiction articles for children's magazines. Formerly a magazine editor in New York, her essays have appeared in publications such as the *New York Times* and the *Christian Science Monitor.* Susan collects antiquarian children's books and participates in a weekly children's writers' group. She is a member of the Society of Children's Book Writers and Illustrators.

PHOTO ACKNOWLEDGMENTS

The images in this book are used with the permission of: Mark Twain House, Hartford, CT, pp. 2, 10, 22, 33, 42, 69, 74, 81, 82, 86, 90, 92, 99; The Mark Twain Project, The Bancroft Library, pp. 6, 28, 39, 57, 58, 97; Fred Green Carpenter/Federal Writers and Artists Project, p. 13; Library of Congress, pp. 16, 49; Frances F. Palmer/Currier & Ives, Publisher. *A Midnight Race on the Mississippi.* Colored lithograph. 1860. Museum of the City of New York. Harry T. Peters Collection, 58.300.24, p. 25; North Wind Picture Archives, p. 30; The Mariners' Museum, Newport News, VA, p. 40; Nevada Historical Society, p. 47; Frances Loeb Library, Graduate School of Design, Harvard University, p. 72; © Bettmann/Corbis, p. 85.

Cover Photos
Hardcover: Hannibal Convention and Visitor's Bureau, front; Mark Twain House, Hartford, CT, back.
Softcover: Nevada Historical Society, front; The Mark Twain Project, The Bancroft Library, back.